Accounting for Business Success

Transforming Your Garbage Into Treasure

- Understand accounting without a college degree

- Discover what your financial statements are telling you

- Use the financial information to improve your business

Michael R. Allen
**Founder, President, and Chief Creative
Officer of Allen & Company, PC CPA Firm**

Published by Michael Allen, Kennesaw, Georgia.

Michael Allen
1350 Wooten Lake Road, NW
Suite 206
Kennesaw, GA 30144
(770) 428-6229
(770) 425-5481
mallen@allenandcompanypc.com
www.allenandcompanypc.com

Library of Congress Cataloging-in-Publication Data

Allen, Michael.

Michael Allen

Accounting for business success ： transforming your garbage into treasure / Michael Allen.

    p. cm.

ISBN 979-8-9991604-0-9

1. Business-Handbooks, manuals, etc. 2. Accounting-Handbooks, manuals, etc. 3. Budgeting and Forecasting-Handbooks, manuals, etc.

First edition, 2025.

Printed in the United States of America.

Table of Contents

Accounting for Business Success

1 - Introduction

An Accounting Poem

In times of war, businesses need monthly accounting
In times of peace, businesses need monthly accounting
In times of economic downturn, businesses need monthly accounting
In times of prosperity, businesses need monthly accounting

A Growing Trend of Indifference

Despite the need for businesses in having monthly accounting, less than 25% of businesses with less than 500 employees actually have financial statements of any kind, according to the Federal Reserve Board's National Survey of Small Business Finances.

Have you ever ridden the Space Mountain ride at Magic Kingdom? You climb up a 180-foot mountain and then blast off into outer space. All you see is the remote blackness of the dark universe, illuminated only by shooting stars and satellites. You never know which way you are going to turn or drop. Do you remember that feeling? You're scared, but laughing uncontrollably at the same time.

I meet business owners who run their businesses in the same way. Once upon a time, there was a business that sold athletic shoes and the owner of this business didn't bother to prepare financial statements of any kind. Instead, he thought that merely keeping an eye on the bank account balance from time to time would be good enough. He actually had no idea how his business was performing and couldn't see where the business was going. He was living in remote blackness, illuminated only by passing crises. More on this business later.

Consequences of Indifference

Yes, I know what you're thinking. Many small businesses use accounting software for their accounting. They believe that by simply using the software that they'll get accurate information about their business.

In my experience, they may use accounting software to create sales invoices and they may also print checks to pay their vendors. Many of these businesses never reconcile their bank statements or even look at their income statement. And who knows - they might even stop after downloading their banking transactions into their accounting software without making sure the payments are associated with the correct general ledger accounts. In my biased opinion, they may be saving money by not engaging an accounting firm to assist them with their accounting, but they may be doing more damage in the long run to their business in the process.

After all, the most successful businesses outsource what they *don't* do well and focus on what they *do* well in order to prosper.

Many business owners delegate the bookkeeping to an employee or family member with no accounting training at all or even assume it themselves. After all, how hard can the accounting be? My question is, would they also represent themselves in court rather than hiring an attorney or perform minor surgery on themselves rather than consulting a physician? I digress. Even large companies tend to pay the minimum salary to their controllers and accountants, because they don't perceive their value to the business. Some of the bookkeepers in small- and medium-size businesses set up equity accounts as expense accounts and asset accounts as liability accounts and then the business owners are surprised at the end of the year when their tax preparer tells them that their taxable income on their tax return is much different from the net income reported on their software's income statement.

Which leads me to one of my sayings: "Some business owners have no business being in business." But I know this isn't you.

Worse than delegating the bookkeeping to Uncle Theo sitting in his garage workshop is not having financial statements at all. Remember that athletic shoe business I mentioned earlier? The business owner didn't concern himself with having financial statements prepared and, instead, kept a watchful eye on the bank account to make sure there was a positive cash balance.

Well, the business rocked along all year making good money and then spending most of it. At the end of the year, a tax return was prepared with a summary schedule of income and expenses. The owner had no idea what the net income was nor the income tax liability. It turned out that the owner owed $36,000 to the Internal Revenue Service (IRS) and had to enter into an installment agreement to begin paying off the balance, including interest and penalties. Without financial statements during the year, tax planning couldn't be performed either, which would have at least given the owner some time to conserve cash or implement tax savings strategies.

Most business owners, including you most likely, work harder than any of their employees and make less income than they could make elsewhere. Why? Most people start a business to have more freedom or to know that they're in control of their future. Yet many business owners let their businesses run them instead of them running their businesses. In fact, they end up with a *job*, the very thing they didn't want. [1]

Around 80% of businesses that start each year fail in the first five years. Of those that survive, 80% of them will fail in the next five years. If I did my math right, that means that only 4% of the original businesses will succeed. With so much information available on how to succeed in business, why are so few businesses succeeding? Well, unfortunately, that's a topic for another book. [2]

The Importance of Accounting for Your Business

What I do know is that accurate financial statements are part of the foundation of a successful business. It is vitally important for your business to have accurate financial statements so that you know where your business stands at any point in time. The progress of your business is recorded in your accounting reports.

Financial statements will help you make better decisions. Financial statements are historical, but they can be very meaningful in helping business owners make informed business decisions about the future. Financial statements are a tool for managing your business and making informed business decisions.

Additionally, financial statements are a starting point for income tax planning. I admit, tax planning seems boring, but if you purposefully implement tax strategies to reduce taxable income and, therefore, the related income taxes, you'll have that much more cash to pay yourself or reinvest into the business.

But simply having accurate financial statements does no one any good unless the business owners understand what they reveal about their businesses. Not only should the financial statements be accurate and understood, they should be timely so that the business owner can change marketing strategies if the current ones aren't producing the desired sales. If you find out in the ninth month of the year that the thousands of dollars spent on marketing campaigns have done absolutely nothing, it's a bit too late to overcorrect for the year by changing marketing plans in the last three months. With recent financial statements, you can also react to overspending and start reducing expenses before it's too late.

The following are just a few questions that can be answered by understanding your financial statements:

- How much is due from customers?
- Is there enough cash to pay amounts due to vendors?
- Is inventory being sold frequently enough?
- Are bank loans helping to increase sales?
- What products or services are profitable or losing money?
- What expenses are too high and out of control? [3]

Accounting vs. Bookkeeping

Bookkeeping is not the same as accounting. Bookkeeping is the record-keeping part of the accounting process. Accounting includes bookkeeping, but it comprises many more complex activities that require a great deal of education, training, judgment, and knowledge of business. Accounting encompasses activities such as preparing financial statements, making informed estimates, budgeting, forecasting, and interpreting financial statements. [4]

Purpose of This Book

The purpose of this book is to help business owners, their managers, and their bookkeepers attain a basic understanding of how to perform accounting and prepare accurate and timely financial statements without formal education or training. You will learn the basic components of financial statements, understand the recording and closing processes, and most importantly, discover how to interpret what financial information is telling you about your business. You'll also learn how to prepare budgets and cash forecasts to keep your business moving according to your plans and goals. (You have developed plans and goals haven't you?) Through this process, you'll actually be creating a system that anyone in the organization can follow so that as a business owner, ultimately you can have the information needed to make better business decisions and *cause* the business to succeed.

I'm a Certified Public Accountant (CPA) and majority owner of an accounting firm that provides accounting, tax, and consulting services. Why would I write a book with information about how businesses can do their own accounting? The short answer is that our accounting firm cannot seem to annihilate the business accounting software industry.

The long answer is that, in this age of technology, we've seen more and more small- and medium-size businesses attempt to do their own accounting with disastrous results rather than to outsource it to professionals who really know what they're doing and who can help them improve the financial information they need to propel their businesses. As a result, the monthly and quarterly accounting work in accounting firms is evolving into annual work only and business owners and managers do not have accurate financial information throughout the year on which to base their decisions.

Businesses still need CPAs to help them navigate the complex tax law and prepare income tax returns after each year-end. As part of preparing the income tax returns, accountants must review their clients' general ledgers and propose correcting and reclassifying journal entries so that the information is correct and presentable on the income tax returns. Unfortunately, the corrected financial information is then too late for decision-makers in the businesses to rely upon.

Over the years, I've seen many of the financial statement amounts reported in the wrong places and transactions posted to the wrong accounts. For example, Accumulated Depreciation is an account that accumulates the depreciation expense deducted over the years and is a "contra asset account" that should be reported as a negative amount below the original cost of a company's Fixed Assets in order to reflect the net depreciated cost of those assets. I've seen a financial statement that was supposedly audited by a CPA firm where this Accumulated Depreciation account was reported as a liability account instead along with Accounts Payable. I've also seen loan payments recorded as expenses when the loan principal payments should instead reduce the loan liability balance.

So let me help you help me. If I can help business owners prepare reasonably accurate financial statements so they can interpret the information and make good business decisions throughout the year, then my time has been worthwhile. If I can help business owners provide reasonably accurate financial statements to their accountants so that they can reduce their time spent on accounting adjustments and spend more time preparing income tax returns and providing business advice, then I have in a small way contributed in making the world a better place.

One Last Thing Before We Begin

Before moving on to the next chapter, let me suggest that you engage a CPA firm to assist you with your business accounting and preparation of your financial statements. Don't spend your valuable time or that of your employees' by struggling with accounting. Focus on what you do well and make money for your business and for yourself. Let the accounting professionals do what they do well. They will partner with you and hold you accountable. They will help you understand where your business stands and how you can get it to where you want it to be.

The best accountant and advisor will help you dream about both your business and personal goals and then develop a strategy to achieve them. They will help you increase sales, decrease expenses, increase cash flow by minimizing income taxes, develop a culture of winning, create a team that works great together, and create systems so that the business can eventually run without you. Yes, you read that right - run without you. The best accountant and advisor will ultimately help you build a successful business that you can sell one day for its highest price or turn over to one of your children.

Okay. I see that you haven't yet outsourced your business accounting to a CPA firm and would rather keep the joy of the accounting function to yourself.

The beauty of this book, if I say so myself, is that you'll be receiving a condensed college education and the equivalent of a bachelor's degree in accounting without spending thousands of dollars. You'll also gain the experience of an accountant and controller without going through the painful interview process, putting up with dumb jokes from colleagues, sitting through endless meetings, attending three-day ropes courses in an effort to build team unity, and fighting over that last Cal-Mex burrito provided by the caterer. I digress.

Where was I? Oh, the beauty of this book is also that it can be used as a reference manual with step-by-step instructions so that anyone in your organization can theoretically follow the steps and produce the information required by the owners and managers to make good business decisions.

Accounting Defined

Accounting is the language of business. The concepts and techniques of accounting make it possible to translate business activity into monetary terms so that the financial transactions of the business can be recorded, summarized, evaluated, and communicated.

Accounting has been defined as "the art of recording, classifying, and summarizing in a significant manner and in terms of money, transactions and events which are, in part at least, of a financial character, and interpreting the results thereof." [1]

13

Financial statements are the result of the financial accounting process. Their general purpose is to communicate certain kinds of financial accounting information to users. The three primary financial statements include the following:

- Balance Sheet – Presents information about the financial position (ending balances of assets, liabilities, and equity, i.e.) of an entity at a particular date. The balance sheet is usually prepared as of the close of business on a particular day.
- Income Statement – Presents the results of operations (income and expenses, i.e.) of an entity for a particular period of time. The period can be a year, a quarter, or a month.
- Statement of Cash Flows – Provides information about cash received and paid out and information about financing and investing activities during a particular time period. [2]

Be aware that a separate Statement of Retained Earnings can be prepared that reflects the changes in equity during the period (capital invested, dividends paid, and net income or loss, e.g.). However, such changes can also be reported in the equity section of the Balance Sheet and, for the purposes of this book, we assume that such changes are reported on the Balance Sheet for simplicity.

In the next chapter, we'll discuss the balance sheet and describe each of the accounts affecting it.

3 – Understanding Balance Sheet Accounts

Some business owners are only aware of an income statement, but, yes, there is also a balance sheet as part of the financial statements. Why is a balance sheet important? Because it reflects the financial health of a business. It reports the assets owned by the company, the liabilities owed to others, and the net worth of the company (assets net of liabilities).

In this chapter, we'll discuss the different sections of the balance sheet, their relationship to the other sections, and the various balance sheet accounts.

The Balance Sheet Components

The balance sheet is divided into three main sections, including assets, liabilities, and equity. Assets are economic resources or things of value owned by a business. They have value in the benefits they can provide. Liabilities are amounts a business owes to others. Equity represents the assets remaining to the owners after liabilities have been paid. [1]

Assets can be further classified as either current or noncurrent. Current assets include receivables, inventory, temporary investments, and other assets that be converted into cash within a year. [2] Liabilities, too, can be further classified as either current or long-term. Current liabilities include accounts payable, accrued liabilities, customer deposits, and other liabilities that will be paid within one year. [3]

The Accounting Equation

The liabilities and equity of a business represent claims against all of the assets. Therefore, the basic accounting equation can be expressed as follows:

Assets = Liabilities + Equity

Or stated another way:

Assets – Liabilities = Equity

Think of equity as the net assets remaining after the liabilities have been paid. Any increase or decrease in assets results in a corresponding increase or decrease in liabilities or equity or both. The two sides of the equation must always be equal. [4]

Cash is King

Cash is also known as currency, because it flows in and it flows out. Cash is totally safe from loss of principal and includes checking accounts, savings accounts, certificates of deposit, and treasury bills. [5]

Cash is king for any business! It stabilizes the business's portfolio and must be on hand to meet daily expenses. Cash balances should be reported as current assets on the balance sheet.

Cash Does Not Necessarily Equal Net Income

Cash does not necessarily equal net profits. I can't tell you how many times we've prepared an income tax return for a client and this is the first time they've discovered how much net income their business had for that year. That's a topic for another chapter. After recovering from their shock, they inevitably tell me, "Well, why don't we have that much cash in our bank account?" Let me explain:

- Some cash receipts don't affect net income. For example, when a business obtains a working capital loan from a bank, the debt proceeds are not income. The proceeds are a liability reported on the balance sheet, because it is due to be repaid to the lender.
- Some cash disbursements don't affect net income. For example, when a business repays a working capital loan to a bank, the debt principal payments are not expenses. The repayments reduce the liability reported on the balance sheet until the loan is eventually repaid in full. Only the interest portion of the payments are expenses.
- Some income doesn't affect cash. For example, when a business bills a customer for a service sold and doesn't collect payment at the time of sale, the income is recognized and a corresponding accounts receivable is recorded on the balance sheet to reflect the amount due to be collected from the customer. Only when the customer pays is cash received and the receivable amount reduced.
- Some expenses don't affect cash. For example, consider the purchase of equipment by a business with cash. Accounting standards require, in general, that the purchase cost be recorded as an asset on the balance sheet and expensed in the form of depreciation over the useful life of the asset. In the third year that the business owns the asset, no cash has been paid since it was originally purchased in year one, but the business deducts depreciation expense.

Receivables

There are several different types of receivables. Accounts receivable are trade receivables due from customers related to a sale made to them. When a credit sale (a sale not requiring immediate payment, i.e.) is made, a sales invoice is generated and reported as sales income and an accounts receivable is created to reflect the balance due from the customer. Accounts receivable should be reported as current assets since they are due from the customer within 30 to 120 days, depending on the credit terms, or at least in the next 12 months. [6]

A note receivable is a promise in writing from a customer, or the "maker," to pay a fixed amount on demand, by a certain date in the future, or periodically over time. An interest-bearing note receivable specifies both the principal and interest the maker has promised to repay. The short-term portion of the note receivable is the amount of principal due in the next 12 months and should be reported on the balance sheet as a current asset. The long-term portion of the note receivable is the remaining amount of principal due after the next 12 months and should be reported on the balance sheet as a current asset. [7]

Other current receivables include amounts loaned by the business to owners and employees.

Inventory

Inventory includes items held for sale in the ordinary course of business, are in process of production for such sale, or are to be currently consumed in the production of goods to be available for sale. [8]

Inventory is recorded as a current asset on the balance sheet when purchased and it is only expensed as Cost of Goods Sold when it is sold and the related sales invoice is recorded as sales revenue. At that time, the inventory is reduced or "relieved from inventory" and the cost of goods sold is recorded.

Prepaid Expenses

A prepaid expense is recorded as a current asset when a business pays for an expense before it receives the benefit. For example, if a business pays an annual premium on an insurance policy at the beginning of the coverage term, a prepaid expense is initially recorded and, as the policy period passes, the asset balance is decreased and reclassified to insurance expense each period that the business benefits from the insurance coverage. [9]

Investments

Businesses invest cash that they don't need for day-to-day operations in debt or equity securities in order to earn a return on the amount invested. An investment is considered to be temporary if the securities are "readily marketable", or readily salable, and management intends to redeem the investment within a year. Temporary investments should be recorded as current assets and other investments not meeting this criteria should be recorded as noncurrent assets. [10]

Other Current Assets

Other current assets are those assets that can be converted into cash within one year but do not qualify as cash, receivables, inventory, prepaid expenses, or temporary investments.

Fixed Assets

Fixed assets are tangible (touchable or physical, i.e.) assets used in the operations of a business. They usually have long useful lives (the period over which the assets' benefits are received, i.e.) and include automobiles, buildings, equipment, furniture and fixtures, land, leasehold improvements, and signs. [11]

The cost of fixed assets includes all the expenditures necessary to acquire them and get them ready for their intended use. Therefore, cost includes the invoice price, less discounts, plus freight, installation, and sales taxes. [12]

According to the IRS, businesses may simply expense the cost of fixed assets if the purchase price is less than $500 if they don't have audited financial statements and expense fixed assets costing less than $5,000 if they do have audited financial statements. If the cost of fixed assets exceed these thresholds, they must be recorded as assets on the balance sheet and then depreciated over time. Businesses should have a written policy specifying the eligible threshold elected.

Depreciation is the systematic allocation of the cost of *fixed assets* over their useful lives when their benefits are received. As depreciation is recognized each period, it is both expensed in a Depreciation Expense account and accumulated in an Accumulated Depreciation asset "contra" account. [13]

Note that there may be different depreciation methods and useful lives of fixed assets for internal book purposes and income tax purposes. There may also be special tax depreciation deductions available for businesses desiring to reduce their taxable income. Please consult a tax professional to determine if your business has different options to consider.

Intangible Assets

Intangible assets are noncurrent assets that are not tangible or physical. They either represent special rights and privileges protected by law such as patents, copyrights, trademarks, trade names, franchise fees, customer lists, loan origination costs, noncompetition agreements, organization and start-up costs, or goodwill.

Intangible assets should be recorded at their cost of acquisition and amortized over time. [14]

Amortization is similar to depreciation, but is the systematic allocation of the cost of *intangible assets* over their useful lives not to exceed 40 years. Amortization must usually be calculated using the straight-line method. [15] According to the IRS, certain intangible assets are classified as Section 197 intangible assets and must be amortized over 15 years. Examples of Sec. 197 intangible assets are patents, copyrights, noncompetition agreements, franchise fees, trademarks, and trade names.

Other Assets

Other assets are noncurrent assets that do not qualify as current assets, fixed assets, intangible assets, or long-term investments. An example is refundable security deposits at the end of a lease term. [16]

Payables

There are various different types of payables. Accounts payable are trade payables owed for goods, supplies, or services purchased on credit. The amount recorded as an account payable is established by the vendor's invoice. Accounts payable should be recorded as current liabilities since the amount is due to be repaid within 30 to 120 days, depending on the credit terms, or at least in the next 12 months. [17]

The short-term portion of a note payable discussed later is the amount of principal due in the next 12 months and should be reported on the balance sheet as a current liability.

Accrued liabilities are obligations for expenses that have been incurred but have not yet been paid. Certain expenses are incurred continuously, but the payments are only made periodically. For example, purchases made with a credit card must be accrued at the end of the period if the credit card balance isn't paid until the following period. Accrued liabilities include accrued payroll taxes, salaries and wages, commissions, credit card liabilities, dividends or distributions, interest, retirement plan contributions, sales taxes, income taxes, and property taxes. [18]

Now I'd like to take this opportunity to specifically help those who record the payment of net payroll checks or direct deposits and payroll taxes. When using a third-party payroll service, the service usually provides an option for the business to either assume responsibility for remitting the payroll taxes to the government taxing agencies or allowing the payroll service to assume the responsibility and, therefore, draft the business bank account for the taxes owed. Additionally, the business can either issue pay checks or allow employees to have the net pay deposited directly into their bank accounts.

The Payroll Equation

Even when only the net pay is clearing the bank account, both the gross salaries and wages must be recorded as expense and the payroll taxes and other withholdings must be recorded as liabilities. Therefore, the basic payroll equation can be expressed as follows:

Gross Salaries and Wages - Withholdings = Net Pay

Net Pay Must be "Grossed Up"

Please don't take a short-cut and only record the net pay clearing the bank account. Simply recording the net pay understates the gross salaries and wages paid and ignores the liability the business has as the employees' agent in withholding their payroll taxes due to be remitted to the government. The taxes withheld as well as other withholdings should be recorded as accrued liabilities and then reduced or "relieved" when they are, in turn, paid to the government agencies.

The payroll taxes drafted from the bank account by the payroll service represents both the employees' taxes withheld from their paychecks as well as the employer's matching Social Security and Medicare taxes and state and federal unemployment taxes. As stated above, the payment of the employees' payroll taxes already withheld should reduce the accrued liability previously recorded and should not be expensed. I've seen businesses make this error several times in my experience. If the employees' withheld taxes are expensed along with the employer's share of the payroll taxes, the payroll tax expense is almost doubled and leads the unsuspecting business owner to believe that taxable income is much less than it really is.

Sample journal entries are provided in "The Recording Process" Chapter 5 to help you understand the mechanics of these transactions.

Other Current Liabilities

Other current liabilities are those liabilities that must be paid within one year but do not qualify as payables, accrued liabilities, or the current portion of notes payable. An example is refundable tenant deposits (to cover repairs, e.g.) within the next 12 months if not due at the end of a lease term. [19]

Debt

A promissory note is a promise in writing to pay a fixed amount of money on demand or on a certain date. A promissory note is signed by the person making the promise, or the "maker." Such a note payable is considered long-term if the period to maturity exceeds one year. For an interest-bearing long-term note, interest is paid periodically as specified in the note and the principal is paid at maturity. Interest should be accrued at the end of each period. [20]

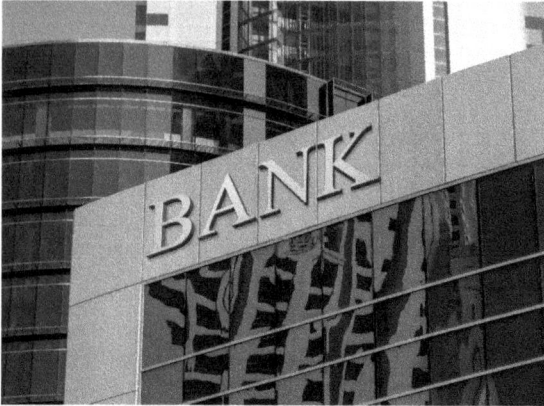

Ownership Shares

The types of investors' ownership shares depends on the legal entity of the business. Corporations issue common stock certificates to their shareholders who purchase the stock.

Some common stock is issued without a face value. If stock does have a face value, it may be either a par value or a stated value. Par value is an arbitrary dollar value for stock specified in a corporation's charter. When a stockholder purchases stock, the business records the cash received and the par value of the shares issued. If the stockholder pays more than the par value of the stock, the excess price is recorded as additional paid-in capital. [21]

Contributed Capital

Contributed capital is the cash or property invested or donated by the investors. [22] Partnerships issue partnership interests to their partners who contribute capital in the form of property or services and thereby purchase their interest. [23] Limited Liability Companies issue member units to their members who contribute capital and thereby purchase their interest.

When a partner or a limited liability company member purchases an ownership interest, the business records the cash received and the capital contributed. Capital contributions are a component of equity on the balance sheet and are not income.

Dividends and Distributions

A dividend is a distribution of profits to stockholders of a regular C corporation. [24] A distribution is, in general, also a distribution of profits to partners of a partnership, [25] to members of a limited liability company, and to shareholders of S corporations. Accordingly, dividends and distributions are equity accounts. Time and time again I've seen businesses set these accounts up as expense accounts instead, which can greatly distort net income.

Owners' Equity

Retained earnings is a component of stockholders' equity in a corporation that reflects the cumulative results of operations retained by the corporation. [26] In other words, retained earnings represent the accumulated profits that the corporation has not paid out to stockholders as dividends but has instead been reinvested in the business.

The capital accounts of partners of partnerships and members of limited liability companies are increased by capital contributions and income and are decreased by capital withdrawals (or distributions) and expenses.

Retained Earnings Does Not Equal Cash

I've had one or two business owners ask me why their retained earnings balance does not equal their cash balance. So I have to believe there are others out there who wonder the same thing. After all, if the business has retained the profit, it should still be in their bank account, right? Wrong. First of all, as was mentioned before, the cash balance in the bank account does not necessarily equal net income. Second, while the net income has not been paid out in dividends or distributions, it was most likely not been kept in the cash account. It was probably reinvested in the business and used to purchase inventory, acquire investments, and purchase equipment or used to pay loans.

In the next chapter, we'll discuss the income statement and describe the primary accounts affecting it.

4 – Understanding Income Statement Accounts

Most business owners are aware of their income statements, because they understand that knowing the business's income and expenses is important. However, some of them have not taken time to understand the various components and what they reveal about their businesses. Do you know which products or services are contributing the most to the sales of your business? Is the gross profit of your business more than the operating expenses so that your business is profitable? Do you know what the fixed operating costs are (expenses that are the same every month, i.e.)? Do you know what the variable operating costs are (expenses that can be changed based on your decision-making and that can fluctuate based on the level of sales, i.e.)?

In this chapter, we'll discuss the different sections of the income statement, their relationship to the other sections, and the various income statement accounts.

The Income Statement Components

In the Bible, the number seven is the number for perfection and completion. The basic income statement, coincidentally, has seven main sections, including sales, cost of sales, gross profit, operating expenses, operating profit, other income and expenses, and net profit. [1]

Of course, a business generates sales by selling goods or services. Cost of sales is the cost of the products or services directly related to their sales. Gross profit is the sales revenue remaining to cover operating costs after deducting the direct costs, such as material purchases and labor. Operating expenses are indirect costs of running the business, such as advertising, insurance, and office supplies. Operating profit is the sales revenue remaining after deducting direct cost of sales and operating expenses. Other income and expenses are those that do not occur during the normal course of operating a business, such as gains from selling equipment. Net profit is the revenue remaining after *all* income and expenses have been accounted for.

Sales

I don't need to elaborate on sales do I? Sales is what the business does and should be one of the primary goals of every business in existence. Now, *increasing* sales is a topic for another book. Sales revenue is the value of what is received from customers for goods or services sold.

Cost of Sales

Cost of sales are the material and labor costs directly related to goods sold. For example, in a franchised fast food restaurant, cost of sales include the food, beverage, packaging, and crew member wages costs.

The Cost of Sales Equation

Cost of sales includes the cost of materials and goods acquired or produced for resale, the cost of labor in providing or producing the goods or services, freight, and the change in inventory during the period. [2] Therefore, the basic cost of sales equation can be expressed as follows:

$$\text{Beginning Inventory} + \text{Purchases} + \text{Labor} + \text{Freight} - \text{Ending Inventory} = \text{Cost of Sales}$$

Gross Profit

If you ask small business owners the difference between gross profit and net profit, you'd be surprised at how many different answers you'd get. They are not the same. Gross profit is the larger number of the two and represents the direct profit of the goods or services sold. It is calculated as the sales revenue minus the cost of sales and it represents the sales revenue remaining to pay operating expenses.

There was once a nice lady who started her own business making and selling perfume. After several months in business, she couldn't understand why the business continued to lose money. It turned out that she hadn't compared the sales price of her products to the costs necessary to make them. Her direct costs were higher than her sales prices! She was actually losing money on every sale. That's why it's important to understand gross profit.

Operating Expenses

Operating expenses are the selling, general, and administrative expenses necessary to run a business. They include expenses such as advertising, executive and administrative salaries and wages, insurance, repairs and maintenance, supplies, telephone, travel, and utilities.

Operating Profit

Operating profit is the profit earned during the normal course of operating a business and is calculated as the sales revenue minus cost of sales and operating expenses. It is the sales revenue remaining after deducting normal costs of the business, but before considering other abnormal income and expenses.

Other Income and Expenses

The income and expenses that don't occur in the normal course of business operation are reported after the operating expenses section of the income statement. For example, a consulting firm doesn't normally sell office equipment and furniture so any gain or loss on such sales are reported separately. Interest income, miscellaneous income, amortization, depreciation, and interest expenses are also included in this category.

Net Profit

Net profit or net income is the "bottom line" profit of the business. It is the revenue remaining after all income has been reported and all expenses have been deducted. This number, ideally, should be positive. If sales revenue is greater than total expenses, the result is a net profit. If total expenses are more than sales, the result is a net loss. Sometimes business owners rejoice when they don't have any net profit, because it's an indication that they won't have to pay any income taxes. However, these people should be afraid, very afraid. They should be concerned that their business isn't making any money. That is, after all, one of the objectives of operating a business.

In the next chapter, we'll discuss the beginning of the accounting process, which is recording the majority of the transactions during the accounting period.

5 – The Recording Process

This is a good place to review and, perhaps, reassess whether you really want to delve deeper into the dark, mysterious underworld of the accounting profession. After all, we've really only swept the surface. We've learned the importance of accounting for your business, discovered the accounting equation, and defined the balance sheet and income statement accounts. But that was all light and fluffy. That was like having a tea party in your three-year old daughter's bedroom.

If we continue, we'll really start getting serious. I mean, there will be dark alleys, smoke-filled rooms, and shady characters. We'll discuss debits and credits, cash basis vs. accrual basis, tax accounting methods, reconciling bank statements, closing the books, interpreting financial statements, and preparing cash flow statements and budgets. This will be no tea party. This will be like having a personnel evaluation with your boss without any tea – or coffee! This will be a gut-check to see if you really have what it takes to do the accounting for your business.

I am pleading with you! Turn back now and let a professional do this complex and thankless work so that you can play golf with a customer and make a sale, have lunch with a vendor and sign an equipment lease, or plan your next shareholders' meeting in Lake Tahoe.

Creating a Chart of Accounts

Alrighty then. Either I cannot write very persuasively to convince you to stop this madness and abandon this "doing your own accounting" idea or you're really enjoying this book. Let's proceed, shall we?

Think of the recording process as organizing all the disorganized transaction activity of the business and ultimately summarizing it into a valuable report to be used as a decision-making tool for the business.

At the foundation of an accounting system is a list of all accounts that a business uses called a Chart of Accounts. Similar to the Dewey Decimal Classification system that organizes books based on subject matter and allows for expansion for further detail, a Chart of Accounts organizes accounts based on type and allows for expansion (for different business locations, e.g.) with extension numbers. While not all accounting software requires that a unique account number be assigned to each account description, it is highly recommended. A sample Chart of Accounts for a corporation is included in Appendix A.

In the sample Chart of Accounts, account names are assigned account numbers.

- Assets accounts: 1000 – 1999
- Liability accounts: 2000 – 2999
- Equity accounts: 3000 – 3999
- Sales accounts: 4000 – 4998
- Cost of Sales accounts: 5000 – 5999
- Operating Expense accounts: 6000 – 6799
- Other Income and Expense accounts: 6800 – 7099
- Passthrough Investment accounts: 7100 – 7999

Accounts listed in a Chart of Accounts are also referred to as general ledger accounts, because they also appear in a General Ledger report when transactions are recorded in those accounts.

Source Documents

Accounting records include source documents that provide evidence of the completed transactions and, therefore, serve as the basis for entries made into the accounting system. The most common source documents needed to begin the accounting procedures include the following:

- Bank statements.
- Cash deposits recorded in a deposits report such as a Cash Receipts Journal.
- Cash disbursements recorded in disbursements reports such as a Check Register and a Cash Disbursements Journal.
- Accounts receivable aging report.
- Inventory list with quantities and extended costs.
- Vendor invoices.
- Accounts payable aging report.
- Payroll journals.
- Credit card statements.
- Sales invoices recorded in a sales report such as a Sales Journal.
- Cash and credit card sales recorded in a point-of-sale system sales report.

You Must Record the History of Your Business

When I became frustrated watching current events unfold and seeing some of the decisions being made by political leaders, I began to study the founding of America and the principles the

Founders believed in and implemented. I learned that I love history. I began reading biographies of American presidents and when I finished reading a biography of our tenth president, John Tyler, I realized that I couldn't remember specific qualities that made him either a great or an average leader. So I began reading those biographies again. And taking notes. Some might say that I re-wrote the books. But I didn't. OK, I may have taken too many notes, but I added headings that titled the following section, underlined significant phrases, bolded sentences referencing original accomplishments, and ensured that the events followed in chronological order.

Where am I going with this? Oh, yes. Just as historians record the events of history, so business owners too must record the history of their businesses. Every year, at a minimum, the Internal Revenue Service requires an income tax return to be filed and your financial statements are the starting point in preparing tax returns. Lenders, too, will periodically require financial statements in order to make a lending decision or to analyze the financial statements and ensure that the borrower is complying with the loan covenants.

Most importantly, though, as has been mentioned before, business owners must have timely and accurate financial statements in order to make the most informed decisions to run their businesses.

Garbage In, Garbage Out

In general, information from the source documents must be recorded correctly into detail journals, updated in the General Ledger, presented in a Trial Balance, and ultimately presented in the financial statements. If the information is recorded incorrectly initially, then the financial statements will be wrong. If the financial statements are wrong, then the wrong decisions will be made by the business owner. Eventually, the business will fail. I don't think I'm being overly dramatic here. Even computer programmers believe "garbage in, garbage out." This simply means that incorrect input data produces incorrect output data, or "garbage."

Fortunately, in accounting, all transactions must balance. Remember the accounting equation?

Assets = Liabilities + Equity

Therefore, if the transaction doesn't balance, at least you'll know something is wrong. More on this later.

The Six-Step Accounting Cycle is as follows: [1]

1. Record accounting transactions into journals.
2. Transfer monthly balances to the General Ledger.
3. Prepare journal entries and enter them into the General Ledger.
4. Prepare a Trial Balance.
5. Prepare the financial statements.
6. Carry forward the balance sheet ending balances to the next period.

Step 1 – Record Accounting Transactions into Journals

Software helps with the recording of transactions, but each transaction is recorded into a "debit" or a "credit" column within a journal. The columns are totaled with the debits equaling credits.

Step 2 – Transfer Monthly Balances to the General Ledger

The monthly balances from the various journals are transferred into a General Ledger, which is organized by account number and in order of the financial statement lines. The General Ledger reflects all of the transactions affecting each account during the period. Again, the debit column total must equal the credit column total.

Step 3 – Prepare Journal Entries and Enter Them into the General Ledger

Any entries that cannot be recorded through the normal journals (sales and purchases journals, e.g.) are entered as journal entries into a General Journal and then updated to the General Ledger. A General Journal is a "catch-all" journal used to record transactions not otherwise recorded in the other journals. Again, the debt column total in the journal entries must equal the credit column total. Do you see a pattern here?

Step 4 – Prepare a Trial Balance

A Trial Balance simply lists each of the account numbers, account descriptions, and their total balances that have been transferred from the General Ledger. Again, the debt column total must equal the credit column total.

Step 5 – Prepare the Financial Statements

Financial statements are prepared from the trial balance, but only present the summarized balances of account categories in a standard format useful for decision-making. For example, a business may have five different bank accounts. While the Trial Balance reports each of the cash accounts along with their balances separately, the Financial Statement reports the sum of the five cash balances in one financial statement line.

Step 6 – Carry Forward the Balance Sheet Ending Balances to the Next Period

The balance sheet ending balances are carried forward to the next period as beginning balances for that period. At the end of the year, the income and expense accounts will be reversed out to zero balances and "closed" to the accumulated equity account such as Retained Earnings. [2]

A Historical Perspective

According to some historians, the early development of accounting dates back to ancient Mesopotamia in 7000 BC where the government began controlling and taxing goods and transactions in the temple economy. [3] However, some religious scholars believe that Adam was not created until just a few years before 4000 BC. In any case, the early Mesopotamians, Egyptians, and Babylonians developed writing, money, counting, and auditing systems to record and monitor the growth of crops and herds. [4]

By 3000 BC, the ruling leaders and priests in ancient Iran charged the people with overseeing financial matters. Consequently, cylindrical tokens were used for bookkeeping on clay scripts and have been found in large rooms for storing crops. Some scripts only contained tables with figures while other scripts also included graphical representations. The invention of a form of bookkeeping using clay tokens was a huge leap forward for mankind and hardly receives enough credit. [5]

There is also evidence of an early form of accounting in the Old Testament. The Book of Exodus describes Moses asking Ithamar to account for materials that had been contributed for the building of the tabernacle. [6]

The historical origin of the use of the words "debit" and "credit" in accounting goes back to the days of single-entry bookkeeping which had the primary objective of keeping track of amounts owed by debtors and amounts owed to creditors. *Debit* in Latin means "he owes" and *credit* means "he trusts." [7]

The earliest evidence of full double-entry bookkeeping appears in the Farolfi ledger of 1299-1300 AD. [8] Florentine merchants in the Giovanni Farolfi & Company acted as moneylenders to the Archbishop of Arles, their most important customer. [9]

Luca Pacioli is recognized as The Father of Accounting and Bookkeeping and was the first person to publish a work on double-entry bookkeeping, which was first published in Venice in 1494 AD. [10]

Understanding Debits and Credits

With a sense of history now, the wise accountants of old agreed to call positive asset balances *debits* and positive liability balances and positive equity balances *credits*. Therefore, the left side of the accounting equation is called the debit side and the right side is called the credit side.

To maintain the balance of the accounting equation, positive debit balances must always equal positive credit balances; that is, debits must always equal credits. This rule is the basis for the double-entry accounting system. This rule is the reason why you cannot exit the entry mode for a journal entry in most accounting software programs until the debits equal the credits.

Debts and credits *within each account* don't have to equal. Only the transaction itself, which may affect multiple accounts, must balance. The difference between total debits and total credits in an account is called the account balance. If the total debits exceed the total credits, the difference is called a debit balance. If the total credits exceed the total debits, the difference is called a credit balance. A normal balance for any account is a positive balance. Therefore, a normal balance for an asset account is a debit balance and a normal balance for a liability or equity account is a credit balance.

The effect of a revenue is to increase equity and the effect of an expense or a withdrawal (dividend or distribution, i.e.) is to decrease equity. Because an equity account is increased by credits and decreased by debits, it follows that a revenue account is increased by credits and decreased by debits. On the other hand, an expense account is increased by debits and decreased by credits.

Be Aware of Bankers

To add to the confusion, just understand that banks use the same terminology of debits and credits. However, the positive balances are reversed. When a bank credits your bank account, they are increasing your balance. This happens when you make a deposit. When a bank debits your bank account, they are decreasing your balance. This happens when you pay a vendor.

To understand this concept, it's helpful to think of the transactions from the bank's point of view. When you deposit your cash in your bank account, the bank also has to consider double-entry bookkeeping. Since your cash does not belong to the bank, it must credit a liability account (called a Deposit on their books) to represent its obligation to you. When you withdraw your cash from your bank account, the bank must debit the Deposit liability account to reduce or "relieve" its obligation to you.

Cash Basis vs. Accrual Basis

Some businesses use the cash basis of accounting while others use the accrual basis of accounting.

The cash basis of accounting records revenue when cash is received and records expenses when cash is paid. However, cash may be received before or after the performance of services of the sale of products. For example, a service or a product may be sold in the current month, but the cash payment may not be collected until the following month. Under the cash basis, the revenue would not be recorded until the following month when the cash is received.

Similarly, under the cash basis, expenses would not be recorded until the cash is paid. Cash payments may be made before or after the consumption of the good or services. For example, if a business pays for liability insurance to cover the next six months, the entire amount would be expensed in the month when paid. The benefits of the insurance coverage, however, are received for the six months of the coverage period. [11]

In an effort to more properly match the revenue to the period when earned and to match the expenses to the period when incurred, the accrual basis of accounting was created. To accrue means to accumulate periodically or to grow.

Under the accrual basis, the timing of cash receipts or cash disbursements is not important in recognizing revenue and expenses. Revenue is recognized when earned or when the earnings process is substantially complete. When a law firm has provided services to a client and issues a sales invoice, the revenue is recognized at that time and an accounts receivable is created for the amount due to be received by the client.

Similarly, under the accrual basis, expenses are recorded when they are incurred in the process of generating revenue. The matching concept requires that expenses are recorded in the same accounting period as the revenue it helped to produce. When a steel manufacturer orders cleaning supplies and receives an invoice, the expense is recognized at that time and an accounts payable is created for the amount due to be paid to the vendor. [12]

While the accrual basis of accounting may the best method to reflect a company's financial position, revenue, and expenses, I did mention that some businesses use the cash basis. This is because the cash basis is, simply put, the simplest accounting method. It is used primarily by small businesses that don't employ accountants to assist them with reporting on the accrual basis. These small businesses are also usually allowed to use the cash basis for income tax return reporting as well.

Income Tax Accounting Methods

For income tax purposes, note that there are strict rules to follow when reporting information on a business income tax return. As a general rule, the Internal Revenue Service requires businesses to use the accrual method of accounting unless it meets an exception to this rule. However, the IRS provides three primary accounting methods that are acceptable, including the following:

1. Accrual Method.
2. Cash Receipts and Disbursements Method.
3. Any other method permitted or required by a specific Internal Revenue Code (IRC) section, such as the percentage-of-completion method for long-term contracts.

A taxpayer's accounting method must be used consistently and must clearly reflect income.

Without getting too technical, the following types of businesses are allowed by the IRS to use the cash basis of accounting:

• Farming businesses.
• Qualified Personal Service Corporations.
• Certain businesses with gross receipts less than certain thresholds.

Even if a business meets one of these exceptions, it may not be able to use the cash method if that method is restricted by other IRC sections. The cash method may *not* be used if one of the following apply:

1. A method other than cash basis is used to regularly calculate book income and no adjustments are made to reconcile book and tax income.
2. Inventory is a material income-producing factor (unless a "gross receipts" exception is met).
3. The IRS has determined that the cash basis does not clearly reflect income.
4. The business engages in certain specific farming activities.
5. The accrual basis is currently being used and the IRS has not consented to a change to the cash basis.

A business may use the cash basis if one of the following gross receipts (revenue, i.e.) exceptions is met:

1. Average annual gross receipts for the three previous years are $1 million or less. Gross receipts include sales (net of returns and allowances), service income, interest, dividends, capital gains, rents, royalties, and any other incidental income. A business can qualify to use the cash basis under this exemption even if inventory is a material income-producing factor.
2. Average annual gross receipts for the three previous years are $5 million or less. Gross receipts include sales (net of returns and allowances), service income, interest, dividends, capital gains, rents, royalties, and any other incidental income. A business *cannot* qualify to use the cash basis under this exemption if inventory is a material income-producing factor.
3. Average annual gross receipts of *qualifying small businesses* for the three previous years are $25 million or less. Gross receipts include sales (net of returns and allowances), service income, interest, dividends, capital gains, rents, royalties, and any other incidental income. A business *cannot* qualify to use the cash basis under this exemption if inventory is a material income-producing factor. Qualifying small businesses generally include the following:
   a. Businesses other than mining, manufacturing, wholesale trade, retail trade, or information industries.
   b. Service businesses.
   c. Businesses that fabricate or modify tangible personal property upon demand according to customer design or customer specifications (window treatment specialists, e.g.).

Businesses allowed to use the cash basis must still account for the cost of product purchased for resale under the accrual method. Therefore, such product cost can only be expensed when the products are sold. [13]

The Accounting Cycle Begins

Now that we understand the purpose of a Chart of Accounts, we know what source documents are, we understand debits and credits, and we can clearly explain the cash and accrual bases to a friend, it's time to actually perform the accounting following the six-step accounting cycle discussed earlier in this chapter. In the example journal entries that follow, note that "DR" is the abbreviation for *debit* and "CR" is the abbreviation for *credit*.

Recording Sales

If you're using accounting software, you're most likely taking advantage of the ability to create sales invoices to bill customers and inputting cash and credit card payments from customers. If you've never thought through the recording aspect of these transactions, allow me to explain what's happening.

In order to bill customers, you had to first add every new customer to your software. When you make a credit sale, you must create a sales invoice by selecting the appropriate customer to bill, selecting the billable items to include on the invoice, and then printing or e-mailing the invoices.

Upon generating the sales invoice, the sale on credit and the customer accounts receivable is recorded in the software and is reflected in the following journal entry:

DR	Accounts Receivable	$ XXX
CR	Sales	(XXX)

Recording Deposits

When you make a cash sale, you must input the customer payment as a deposit in the bank account register or by recording a journal entry reflected as follows:

DR	Cash	$ XXX
CR	Sales	(XXX)

When you collect a cash payment from a customer that you've billed, you must input the deposit in a customer payments application and select the appropriate customer who made payment. This customer payment is reflected in the following journal entry:

DR	Cash	$ XXX
CR	Accounts Receivable	(XXX)

Recording Purchases

Again, if you're using accounting software, you're most likely taking advantage of the ability to input vendor invoices for purchases and issuing checks and inputting other payments to vendors.

In order to pay a vendor, you had to first add every new vendor to your software and complete their contact information as well as assign the appropriate general ledger account number for recording the transactions. When you receive an invoice from a vendor, you must select the vendor in a vendor application; enter the invoice information such as invoice number, invoice date, terms, and amount due; and input payment amounts for one or more general ledger accounts.

Upon saving the invoice, the purchase on credit and the vendor accounts payable is recorded in the software and is reflected in the following journal entry:

DR	Purchases	$ XXX
CR	Accounts Payable	(XXX)

Recording Payments

When you make a cash payment at the time of purchase, you must input the disbursement amount in the vendor application or in the bank account register or by recording a journal entry reflected as follows:

DR	Purchases	$ XXX
CR	Cash	(XXX)

When you pay a vendor invoice that has previously been input in the vendor application and, therefore, for which an accounts payable has been accrued, you must choose to pay the bill and then print the checks or initiate an electronic payment. The vendor payment is reflected in the following journal entry:

DR	Accounts Payable	$ XXX
CR	Cash	(XXX)

Recording Inventory

Your accounting software may or may not have an inventory application. However, if selling inventory is a material income-producing factor in your business – let me say it another way – if your business sells inventory, then you must track inventory items when you purchase them and when you sell them. If you sell inventory and your software does not have an inventory-tracking application, you should purchase an add-on module or acquire new software with this capability.

When your business purchases items for resale, keeps them in inventory, and then sells them, the accounting software can track the number of items in stock and value the inventory after every purchase and sale.

When you purchase inventory, the cost is not recorded as expense right away. In our earlier discussion of the accrual basis of accounting, the expense must be recorded in the same period in which the revenue is recognized. Whether the business uses the overall cash or accrual basis, recognition of the cost of products sold is really on the accrual basis.

When the product is purchased, it is recorded in the inventory asset account. The inventory purchase is reflected in the following journal entry:

DR	Inventory	$ XXX
CR	Cash	(XXX)

When the product is sold, the inventory is reduced or relieved and the cost of the sale can then be recognized.   The inventory sale is reflected in the following journal entry:

DR	Cost of Sales	$ XXX
CR	Inventory	(XXX)

In the next chapter, we'll discuss the accounting closing process just before the financial statements can be prepared.

6 – The Closing Process

Throughout each month, everyone in the business is kind of doin' their thang. The marketing people are publishing ads, attending networking events, and creating marketing campaigns. The sales people are calling prospective customers, knocking on doors, and making sales. The operations people are ordering inventory, ensuring order fulfillment, or performing services. The accounts receivable clerks are creating sales invoices, following up with customers, and recording their payments. The accounts payable clerks are entering vendor invoices and initiating payments for purchases. And if you're the owner of a small business, you might be doing it all.

And the accountants – if you employ them – are doing nothing. Nothing at all, except playing video games on their computers or hand-held devices, walking to the break room while looking down at their cell phones the entire time pretending to be busy, or maybe answering a question from one of the operations managers. Like why their department's labor cost is so high in the previous month. Then the accountant has to do the research, comb through the payroll journals, compare costs to another month, and then finally explain that the operations manager authorized way too much overtime because he or she failed to schedule the operations staff adequately.

It's only at the beginning of the next month, after all of the other people have done their thang in the previous month, when the accountants spring into action and do their magic. The monthly closing process ensures that all transactions affecting the business in the previous month have been or will be recorded correctly. Most transactions have already been recorded in the normal course of business, but some transactions have not yet been recorded and need to be. After ensuring that all transactions have been recorded, the accountant will then prepare a Trial Balance report and "agree the balances" to supporting source documents and schedules. If any balances do not agree, the accountant will then use a General Ledger report to determine whether any incorrect amounts or transactions were recorded in the accounting software.

Finalizing Sales

During the accounting cycle of the previous month, any sales billed to customers were recorded with a corresponding journal entry to accounts receivable. Any payments from those credit sale customers were deposited and recorded with a corresponding journal entry to reduce the accounts receivable balance.

Any cash sales were recorded at the time of sale with a corresponding journal entry to cash.

The only other sales to consider are sales transacted with a point-of-sale (POS) system.

If the transactions are accumulated, summarized, and transmitted automatically to the accounting software periodically, the only step remaining is for the accountant to review the sales reports, press a button, and post the sales and deposit transactions to the accounting software sales journal, cash receipts journal, and general ledger.

If the POS system does not interface with the accounting software and, therefore, the transactions are not transmitted automatically to the accounting software, information from the sales reports must be reported in the accounting software by creating a journal entry similar to the following:

DR	Cash	$ XXX
DR	Discounts	XXX
CR	Sales	(XXX)
CR	Accrued Sales Taxes	(XXX)

In the journal entry above, note that sales taxes were collected from customers at the time of sale, but are not revenue. The business is acting as an agent of the state government and collecting sales taxes for it. Therefore, the amount collected and due to be remitted to the government is recorded as an Accrued Sales Taxes liability. When the business pays the sales taxes to the government, the following journal entry is recorded:

DR	Accrued Sales Taxes	$ XXX
CR	Cash	(XXX)

Finalizing Payroll

The business may process payroll in-house or use a third-party payroll service in making sure employees get paid.

Next to engaging a professional accounting firm, one of the best ways a business can spend its money on operating costs is to hire a third-party payroll service. The payroll service is responsible for issuing the paychecks as well as preparing and filing periodic payroll tax returns and year-end Forms W-2. Just make sure that the company has existed for several years. Everyone and his brother, it seems, is trying to get in on the payroll business so there's a lot of competition. However, many of the newer companies, in my experience, tend to make more mistakes.

During the previous month, if the business processed payroll in-house and, therefore, issued paychecks directly to the employees, a journal entry was created when the checks were printed to record gross salaries and wages expense, the employee payroll taxes withheld as accrued liabilities, and the remaining net check amounts as a reduction in cash. The employer's share of FICA taxes and unemployment taxes will be recorded as expense when the business pays them to the government agencies.

However, if the business uses a third-party payroll service, the payroll service most likely provided the option for the business to have the employees withheld taxes as well as the employer's taxes automatically drafted from the account. When the payroll service assumes this responsibility, they usually also assume responsibility for any late payments, in which case they agree to pay any related late payment penalties and interest. Also, with a payroll service, they usually offer the capability of initiating direct-deposits of paychecks into employees' bank accounts in lieu of issuing paychecks. In this case, during the previous month, no accounting was performed to record these transactions, but the business bank account was drafted for any paychecks clearing, direct deposits of paychecks, and payroll taxes.

To avoid the problems described in Chapter 3, the net pay drafted from the bank account must be "grossed up" so that gross salaries and wages are recorded along with the payroll taxes withheld from employees. If you only record the net pay, salaries and wages are understated. The payment of payroll disbursements (gross salaries and wages) and the related employee taxes withheld may be found in the company totals section of the payroll service's payroll journal and recorded in the following journal entry:

DR	Salaries	$ XXX
DR	Wages	XXX
CR	Accrued FICA Taxes	(XXX)
CR	Accrued Federal Income Taxes	(XXX)
CR	Accrued State Income Taxes	(XXX)
CR	Cash	(XXX)

The payment of payroll taxes (employee taxes withheld and employer taxes) is recorded in the following journal entry:

DR	Accrued FICA Taxes	$ XXX
DR	Accrued Federal Income Taxes	XXX
DR	Accrued State Income Taxes	XXX
DR	Payroll Taxes	XXX
CR	Cash	(XXX)

Reconciling Bank Statements

Now for the dreaded reconciling bank statements step in the closing process. I wouldn't be a good accountant if I didn't teach you how to do this. Because bank statement reconciliations reconcile both the ending bank statement balance to the ending book balance and the beginning book balance to the ending book balance, you can be quite confident that you've accounted for all of the transactions affecting the bank account. If both ending book balances agree to each other, that is.

Step 1 – Reconcile the Ending Bank Balance to the Ending Book Balance

Access your bank statement as soon as you can each month. If you have online access to your account, the bank statement should be available shortly after the last day of the month. To reconcile the ending bank statement balance to the ending book balance, use the following formula:

Ending Balance per Bank	$ XXX
ADD: Deposits-in-Transit	XXX
LESS: Outstanding Checks	(XXX)
Ending Balance per Books	$ XXX

Deposits-in-Transit are deposits made at the bank but haven't yet cleared the bank account per the bank statement. Outstanding checks are checks that you've issued but haven't yet cleared the bank account "per" (according to, i.e.) the bank statement. To ignore deposits-in-transit and outstanding checks and simply record only the deposits and disbursements that cleared the bank account would be like having grits without the cheese or key lime pie without the whipped cream. And it wouldn't be correct. For example, if a company mails a check in the amount of $100,000 to a vendor on the last day of the year, the payment wouldn't be recorded until the following year if outstanding checks are ignored.

Step 2 – Reconcile the Beginning Book Balance to the Ending Book Balance

To reconcile the beginning book balance to the ending book balance, use the following formula:

Beginning Balance per Books	$ XXX
ADD: Deposits	XXX
LESS: Disbursements	(XXX)
Ending Balance per Books	$ XXX

Simple, right? Deposits include sales deposits, reimbursements or refunds of expenses, transfers from other bank accounts, deposit corrections made by the bank, and interest income. Most of these deposits may have already been recorded in the accounting system during the previous month. If some haven't, such as transfers and deposit corrections, a journal entry will need to be recorded.

Disbursements include checks issued, transfers to other bank accounts, check corrections made by the bank, net payroll and payroll taxes drafted, ACH debits, returned deposits due to customer insufficient funds, credit card fees, and bank service fees. Again, most of these disbursements may have already been recorded in the accounting system during the previous month. If some haven't, such as check corrections and ACH debits, a journal entry will need to be recorded.

The ending balance per books in Step 2 should agree to the ending balance per books in Step 1. Also, the ending balance per books should agree to the Trial Balance report. If the balances do not agree, a General Ledger report may be useful to compare the transactions actually recorded to what the bank reconciliation indicates should have been recorded.

When using the bank reconciliation application in accounting software, you will need to do the following:

1. Input the ending balance per the bank statement.
2. Check off each check and other disbursement that cleared the bank account.
3. Check off each deposit that cleared the bank account.
4. Save the bank reconciliation report when there is no difference between the ending book balances.

The following are some examples of journal entries that can be recorded as the bank statements are being reconciled:

Non-Sales Cash Receipts

DR	Cash	$ XXX
CR	Taxes – Property	(XXX)

      To record refund of overpaid property taxes

Transfers Between Bank Accounts

DR	Cash – Savings	$ XXX
CR	Cash – Checking	(XXX)

      To record transfers from the checking account to the savings account

ACH Debits

DR	Bank Service Fees	$ XXX
DR	Credit Card Fees	XXX
CR	Cash	(XXX)

      To record ACH debits from checking account

Finalizing the Balance Sheet Accounts

In finalizing the balance sheet accounts, journal entries are recorded to correct the month-end balances of accounts not previously corrected during the normal accounting cycle during the previous month when finalizing sales, when finalizing payroll, or reconciling bank statements.

The following are some sample journal entries that can be recorded when finalizing the balance sheet accounts:

Prepaid Rent

DR	Prepaid Rent	$ XXX
CR	Rent – Facilities	(XXX)

      To reclassify two months of rent payments paid in advance but previously expensed

Depreciation

DR	Depreciation	$ XXX
CR	Accumulated Depreciation	(XXX)

    To record depreciation for the month

A tax accountant usually maintains Depreciation Schedules created in the income tax software and also updates it at least annually when preparing the business income tax returns. This schedule can be prepared both on a tax basis and a book basis and is very useful in estimating depreciation expense for each month during the next year. Without getting too technical, income tax rules require specific methods in order to claim depreciation expense at a faster rate than the "straight-line" method allowed for book purposes. At a minimum, the business should estimate "straight-line" depreciation by dividing the original cost of the fixed assets by their useful lives. For example, equipment is usually depreciated over five years and furniture is usually depreciated over seven years.

Equipment Purchase

DR	Equipment	$ XXX
CR	Small Tools and Equipment	(XXX)

    To reclassify equipment purchased but previously expensed

Amortization

DR	Amortization	$ XXX
CR	Accumulated Amortization	(XXX)

    To record amortization for the month

Accrued Interest

DR	Interest Expense	$ XXX
CR	Accrued Interest	(XXX)

    To record loan interest due in the following month

<u>Debt</u>

DR	Interest Expense	$ XXX
CR	Note Payable	(XXX)

     To reclassify interest portion of loan payment previously recorded as a reduction in the note payable account

Annually Closing the Temporary Accounts

The temporary accounts include the withdrawal, revenue, and expense accounts. At the end of each annual accounting period only, the balances in these accounts need to be transferred to owners' equity. [1] The purpose of the annual closing process is (1) to clear all temporary accounts of their balances so that the operating activity of the next period may be recorded and kept separate from the activity of the current period, (2) to determine the net income or net loss of the current period, (3) to reflect the resulting net income or net loss of the current period in the accumulated equity account, and (4) to produce an updated balance in the accumulated equity account.

The mechanics of the closing procedure are very simple. The balance of each temporary account is reduced to zero by either debiting the account for an amount equal to its credit balance, as would normally be the case with a revenue account, or by crediting the account for an amount equal to its debit balance, as would normally be the case with an expense account. The offsetting credit or debit is usually made to the accumulated equity account such as Retained Earnings for a corporation. [2]

With most accounting software, this closing procedure is done automatically when the current annual period is changed to the next annual period. However, if the business is a partnership and there is more than one partner, withdrawals and net income or loss may need to be specially allocated based on their ownership percentage or profit and loss sharing percentage as defined in the partnership agreement.

Using the Trial Balance

After preparing and recording the journal entries for the accounting period, a Trial Balance report can then be prepared. Many business owners aren't aware of this report, but the Trial Balance is your friend. The Trial Balance will help you determine if the accounting is correct and complete. Some accounting software places the Trial Balance within the Accountant and Taxes reports section. Most business owners, and even some bookkeepers for that matter, don't think of themselves as accountants (nor should they) and, as a result, never even look in this report section. Not even out of curiosity. They see a Company and Financial reports section and only access the income statement – and possibly, every new moon, the balance sheet.

A Trial Balance is similar to a Chart of Accounts, except that it provides the ending balance for each account. The accounts are listed in the order that they appear in the Chart of Accounts as well as in the General Ledger Report, with assets listed first, followed by liabilities, equity, revenues, and expenses. [3]

To determine whether the accounting is correct and complete, you should agree the balance sheet account ending balances per the Trial Balance to the supporting documents and schedules. If the balance sheet account balances agree to the supporting documents and schedules, you can be reasonably assured that the related revenue and expense transactions have been recorded properly. The following are examples of the Trial Balance accounts and their related supporting documents:

Trial Balance Account	Supporting Document or Schedule
Cash	Bank Reconciliation
Accounts Receivable	Accounts Receivable Ledger
Inventory	Inventory Listing
Prepaid Expenses	Prepaid Expenses Schedule
Fixed Assets	Depreciation Schedule
Intangible Assets	Depreciation Schedule
Accounts Payable	Accounts Payable Ledger
Accrued FICA Withholding	Accrued Payroll Worksheet
Accrued Credit Card Liabilities	Credit Card Statement
Accrued Sales Taxes	Sales Tax Return
Note Payable	Loan Amortization Schedule
Common Stock	Stock Ledger

Using the General Ledger

Every transaction recorded is transferred to the General Ledger report. This process is called "posting." The General Ledger is automatically updated in accounting software when a transaction is recorded. Like the Chart of Accounts and the Trial Balance, the accounts are listed in order of assets first, followed by liabilities, equity, revenue, and expenses. [4]

When attempting to agree a balance per the Trial Balance to the supporting document or schedule and the balance doesn't agree, the General Ledger is very helpful in determining what went wrong. This report, like the Trial Balance report, is usually hidden away in an Accountants and Taxes report section. Don't be afraid to look in this section to find the General Ledger report. The General Ledger is very useful because you can see each debit and credit entry posted to each account. You may find that an amount was recorded incorrectly, that it should have been recorded as a debit rather than as a credit, or that it wasn't recorded at all. Once you know what needs to be corrected, prepare and record an adjusting journal entry.

Do you know that young auditors straight out of college and working at a CPA firm will often learn how "to read" a General Ledger as one of their first tasks assigned? They will participate in a financial statement audit of one of their clients and will be asked to review postings in the client's General Ledger. They may simply be looking for transactions that were recorded incorrectly or they may be looking for an attempt by the client's management to conceal an improper transaction.

Now that you know how to read a General Ledger, you don't have to participate in a CPA firm audit, pick up a sandwich every day for the senior in-charge accountant, go to a 5:30 A.M. inventory observation, or endure incredibly negative performance evaluations meant to humble you into submission, break your will, and give you a new identity.

After ensuring that each of the balance sheet account balances per the Trial Balance is correct and agrees to a supporting document or schedule, you can then review the transactions in the revenue and expense accounts to determine if any transactions were recorded incorrectly. Most sales recorded through the accounts receivable billing application will be recorded correctly as well as the purchases recorded through the inventory application. Some examples of common "mispostings" are the following:

Michael Allen

General Ledger Account	Potential Misposting
Charitable Contributions	Employee bonuses not processed as payroll
Computer Expenses	Computer equipment that should be capitalized as an asset
Education and Training	Employee golf green fees
Employee Benefits	Movie theater tickets
Insurance – Group Health	Stockholder health insurance premiums
Miscellaneous	Everything imaginable (transactions recorded in this account should be kept to a minimum, if not zero)
Office Supplies	Equipment and furniture that should be capitalized as an asset
Repairs and Maintenance	Significant repairs that extend the life or increase the value of property or equipment that should be capitalized as an asset
Small Equipment	Equipment that should be capitalized as an asset
Supplies	Equipment that should be capitalized as an asset
Taxes - Other	Personal income taxes paid by the business for the owners that should be recorded as dividends or distributions
Uniforms	Clothing that is not special-purpose clothing for the business that can be worn as personal ordinary-use clothing
Distributions	Distributions are not an expense. This account is an equity account.

Please allow me to vent some frustration about one of the above accounts – Distributions. Some small businesses set up the Distributions account as an expense account. After recording $100,000 of distributions during the year, they mistakenly believe that their taxable income is $100,000 less than it really is. Then they're surprised and angry at the tax accountant who politely informs them at the end of the year that they owe much more tax than they expected.

Some small businesses record distributions in the Officer Salaries account. Similarly, after recording $100,000 of distributions as a payroll expense during the year, they too are bewildered and infuriated at the nice tax accountant who has relayed the message of higher income taxes.

Know this: correct accounting matters. If done incorrectly, it can result in misinformation at the least and wreck families at the most extreme level. Who hasn't heard of the sneaky business owner who inflates deductions or conceals income in order to evade income taxes? Then the IRS conducts an audit and assesses unpaid taxes, penalties, and interest for several years. This leaves the sweet and innocent spouse with a substantial share of the financial burden as well as resentment to the other for not reporting the information correctly in the first place.

Let me now suggest that you buy a "Hug Your Accountant" T-shirt. If your business engages a professional accountant throughout the year, he or she is like James Bond, rescuing you time after time behind the scenes and unknown to you. Accountants step in front of the lethal bullet by reclassifying incorrect amounts, employing karate by ensuring a bank loan with accurate financial statements, and deploying tear gas from a fountain pen by preventing an IRS audit red flag.

In the next chapter, we'll discuss how you can actually understand what the financial statements are telling you about your business and how to start running your business based on the information learned from them.

7 – Understanding Financial Statements

It is important to understand that a Trial Balance is not a financial statement. It is intended primarily for use by accountants when ensuring that the balances are accurate. Once the Trial Balance is correct, financial statements can be prepared, which summarize the balances reflected on the Trial Balance.

In this chapter, we'll discuss the purpose of the balance sheet and the income statement, how to interpret the financial statements, using Key Performance Indicators to view your business as your customers do, and different levels of financial statement quality assurance services that can be provided by CPA firms and other accounting and bookkeeping firms.

Balance Sheet

A Balance Sheet is a financial statement intended for the use of others in making decisions about the business. Its purpose is to show the financial position of a business at a point in time. The Balance Sheet only reflects summary balances of assets, liabilities, and equity accounts and does not reflect revenue and expense account balances. Accordingly, while the Trial Balance reflects every account and its balance, the Balance Sheet only reflects summarized accounts and their balances. For example, four different accrued payroll tax account balances on the Trial Balance will be combined into one Accrued Payroll Taxes balance on the Balance Sheet.

In a "classified" Balance Sheet, assets and liabilities are further classified according to their life span or the way in which they are used. [1] Current Assets include cash, accounts receivable, employee advances, inventory, prepaid expenses, and short-term investments because they are cash or can be converted into cash within one year. Fixed Assets include automobiles, buildings, equipment, furniture and fixtures, land, leasehold improvements, signs, and software because they are used in the operations of the business and have long useful lives. Other Assets include intangible assets, security deposits, and long-term investments because they don't qualify as either current assets or fixed assets. Current Liabilities include accounts payable, accrued liabilities, customer deposits, and short-term portions of debt because they will be paid within one year. Long-term Liabilities include long-term portions of debt because they will be paid beyond one year.

Income Statement

An Income Statement is a financial statement also intended for the use of others in making business decisions. Its purpose is to report the results of operations of a business for a period of time. The Income Statement only reflects balances of revenue and expense accounts and does not reflect asset, liabilities, or equity account balances.

Interpreting Financial Statements

Obtaining a basic understanding of Balance Sheet and Income Statement accounts is important. Understanding the recording and closing process is also important. However, none of the accounting is really important. That is, unless the business owners and managers actually use the end product, the financial statements, to make better decisions about the business.

Consider Warren Buffett. He is considered by some to be one of the most successful investors in the world. In recent years, he was the second wealthiest person in the United States and the fourth wealthiest in the world with a total net worth over $80 billion. [2] Now this is one guy who understands financial statements. He analyzes and interprets financial statements of a business in determining whether to invest in it or not. He also considers what the business does and invests based on a belief in the company's products or services.

Before discussing how to analyze financial statements, be aware that there are limitations to such analysis. Balance sheets are prepared as of a particular date and, therefore, may not indicate financial position at other times during the period. Financial statements are also prepared using different methods of accounting, which can decrease the comparability. Additionally, some companies' financial statements are consolidated and involve many different types of businesses, which make comparisons more difficult. [3]

If you find analysis of financial statements too time-consuming or difficult, please consider asking an accounting professional to assist you. See Appendix B for an additional resource to help you understand the financial health of your business with a plain-language, comprehensive report.

Business owners should read their financial statements and analyze them as follows:

Step 1 – Analyze at a High Level

- High-level financial statement analysis enables a business owner to quickly determine the overall financial health of his or her business before delving into deeper analysis.
- Compare total assets to total liabilities. **HINT:** Total assets should exceed total liabilities.
- Compare current assets to current liabilities. Also known as liquidity, this comparison indicates whether there are enough current assets to pay current liabilities. Cash on

hand, cash collected from customer accounts receivable, and cash collected from sales of inventory should be sufficient to pay accounts payable, accrued liabilities, and current portions of debt due.

- Compare the change in gross fixed assets (before deducting accumulated depreciation) in the current period to the prior period in relation to the change in net profit in the current period to the prior period. **HINT:** As gross fixed assets increase, net profit should increase at an equal or greater rate. Otherwise, the business is not managing its fixed assets effectively.
- Compare the change in total debt in the current period to the prior period in relation to the change in sales revenue in the current period to the prior period. **HINT:** As debt increases, sales should increase at an equal or greater rate. Otherwise, the business is not managing its debt properly.
- Compare the change in the total number of employees in the current period to the prior period in relation to the change in net profit in the current period to the prior period. **HINT:** As the total number of employees increases, net profit should increase at an equal or greater rate. You guessed it; otherwise, the business is not hiring and managing its employees effectively.
- Compare sales revenue in the current period to the prior period. **HINT:** Sales should increase from one period to the next. If they don't there should be a good explanation and a strategy to correct the trend.
- Compare net income in the current period to the prior period. **HINT:** Net profit should increase from one period to the next or, at a minimum, remain stable. If net profit does not at least remain stable, there may be a problem controlling cost of sales or operating expenses.

Step 2 – Analyze Horizontally

- A basic analytical procedure is comparing dollar and percentage changes from one year to the next for each line item in financial statements.
- Compare both the dollar amount and percentage changes for each line item in comparative financial statements (balance sheets and income statements) that include at least two periods. **TIP:** If a zero or negative balance for a line item appears in the first of the two periods being compared, it becomes difficult to compare the two periods. For example, a percentage change cannot be calculated with a base year amount of zero. **EXAMPLE:** If accounts receivable increased by $100,000 and 40% from the previous period, there may be a problem with customer collections.
- Compare the percentage changes for each line item in comparative financial statements that include more than two periods. This "trend analysis" is a type of horizontal analysis that uses one base year to determine the percentage change trend for each line item. [4] **EXAMPLE:** If sales decreased 5% for three years in a row, there may be a problem with advertising, marketing, or even a product line.

Step 3 – Analyze Vertically

- Vertical analysis compares each line item in a financial statement to a common or base amount in the statement and expressed as a percentage of that base amount.
- Compare each line item in a balance sheet and income statement as a percentage of the base amount. Total assets is usually the base amount for the balance sheet vertical analysis and net sales is usually the base amount for the income statement.
  EXAMPLE: If cost of sales within the company has historically been 40% of net sales, but the percentage is now 60%, there may be a problem with inventory waste, vendor price increases, over-ordering, or even employee theft.
- Compare each line item in a balance sheet and income statement as a percentage of the amount to the industry average percentage. [5] **EXAMPLE:** If liability insurance is 3% of net sales but the industry average is only 1%, the company should obtain bids from at least three insurance carriers and attempt to reduce insurance premiums.

Step 4 – Analyze Ratios

- Ratio analysis measures relationships between financial statement amounts. In the equations that follow, the forward slash symbol "/" indicates division in mathematics.
- Compare "effect ratios" to industry average ratios to determine the *extent* of a company's problems.
  - o The Current Ratio (current assets/current liabilities) indicates the amount of liquid current assets available to meet current obligations. **HINT:** A desirable "rule of thumb" current ratio is 2:1.
  - o The Quick Ratio ([cash + short-term investments + net accounts receivable]/current liabilities) also measures liquidity like the current ratio above does, but assumes that no additional inventory can be sold to meet current obligations. **HINT:** A desirable "rule of thumb" quick ratio is 1:1.
  - o The Inventory to Working Capital Ratio (inventory/[current assets – current liabilities]) measures the dependency of working capital on inventory.
    EXAMPLE: If the ratio becomes too large, the business becomes more susceptible to problems caused by inventory that doesn't sell.
  - o The Trade Accounts Receivable to Working Capital Ratio (accounts receivable/[current assets – current liabilities]) measures the extent of the company's reliance on receivables for its working capital. **EXAMPLE:** If the ratio becomes too large, the quality of the company's liquidity is poor.
  - o The Debt to Assets Ratio (debt/total assets) measures financial risk. This ratio primarily determines a company's eligibility for a new loan with a favorable interest rate.
  - o The Net Profit to Net Worth Ratio (net profit/total equity) measures the return on the equity investment in the company. **EXAMPLE:** If this ratio is too high, then the business is using too much debt and too little equity.
- Compare "causal ratios" to industry average ratios to determine *why* the financial statements are changing.

- o The Fixed Assets to Net Worth Ratio (gross fixed assets/total equity) measures the extent to which the owner's equity is tied up in permanent depreciable property and measures the amount of capital that remains for investment in liquid assets. **EXAMPLE:** If too much net worth is tied up in fixed assets, the business will have too little working capital, will over-utilize debt, and profitability will suffer. If profits are not sufficient, then outside equity will be required so that the company may grow without "growing out of business." In some cases, the solution may be to reduce expansion.
- o The Collection Period (accounts receivable/[net sales/365]) measures the collection efficiency of the company. **EXAMPLE:** If this collection period is too high, it can indicate ineffective accounts receivable collection policies. The company may need to obtain a loan to finance the increase in accounts receivable due to having less cash, which may in turn reduce the company's ability to obtain future debt financing.
- o The Inventory Turnover Ratio (net sales/inventory) measures the number of times inventory is sold during the period. **EXAMPLE:** A low ratio indicates slow-moving or obsolete inventory, excessive inventory purchases, or even a poor physical layout of the warehouse and storage areas.
- o The Net Sales to Net Worth Ratio (net sales/total equity) measures the extent to which sales volume is supported by invested capital. **EXAMPLE:** A low ratio indicates that sales should be increased and a high ratio indicates that the business has expanded without investing new capital. Business expansion without new capital may indicate that the company is burdened with excessive debt or may be too dependent on the existing employee base.
- o The Net Profit Margin (net profit/net sales) measures the percentage of net sales kept by the business as profit. **EXAMPLE:** If the net profit percentage is too low, the business must either generate more sales or reduce expenses. However, there is a limit to the amount that expenses may be reduced without negatively affecting the company's quality of business.

Consider a Weekly Report

With the accounting skills developed by reading this book, your business may go from having quarterly, annual, or, no financial statements to monthly financial statements. Now imagine having some key financial information *every week* to understand your business that much sooner! Restaurants use a weekly profit and loss report to identify trends, anticipate problems, capitalize on opportunities, and improve their business every week. There is no reason why your business can't do the same.

The weekly profit and loss report reflects daily sales, cost of sales, and profit compared to budgeted amounts. It also reflects labor hours scheduled, worked, and overtime. This weekly report is designed to be available to management within 24 hours after the end of each week. Small problems can have big effects on profits if not detected early. Similarly, small improvements can improve profits quickly. [6]

Assume a manager or business owner reviews the weekly profit and loss report and discovers a 2% increase in cost of sales. That may not seem like a huge increase, but it also decreases net profit by 2%. He or she then determines that the problem is due to new staff who aren't familiar with the purchasing guidelines and has ordered too much inventory. Management can now conduct several training sessions to ensure that the staff are aware of and complying with the standards. Improvements should be seen in the cost of sales percentage the very next week.

Net profit as a percentage of sales for the week should be compared to the prior week, prior month-end, and budgeted profit percentage. The report provides a quick indication of whether the desired level of profitability is being achieved, corrective measures implemented in prior weeks are working, and whether an adverse trend is occurring that is reducing profitability.

Direct material costs as a percentage of sales for the week should be compared to the prior week, prior month-end, and budgeted cost percentage. These costs along with direct labor are really the only major expenses that can be controlled on a week-to-week basis. Therefore, if quick profit improvement is needed, adjustments to lower these costs are the only real options.

Sales for the week should be compared to the prior week, prior month-end, and budgeted sales. This comparison provides an indication of whether the business is achieving its growth objectives.

Finally, labor amounts, regular hours worked, and overtime hours worked should be compared to the prior week, prior month-end, budgeted labor, and scheduled labor hours to determine whether staff scheduling is as efficient as possible.

Break-Even Point

The break-even point is the level of activity for a period at which the revenues produced by a business activity equal the cost incurred. In other words, it is the level of activity at which there is neither profit nor loss. [7]

Business owners can use break-even analysis in a variety of ways in making decisions. For example, a business that is thinking about adding a new product can determine the number of units needed to sell in order to break even as represented by the following equation:

$$\text{Break-Even Sales Units} = \frac{\text{Fixed Expenses}}{(\text{Sales Price per Unit} - \text{Variable Expenses per Unit})}$$

For example, if the selling price of a proposed product is $50, the variable cost per unit is $30, and the fixed expenses are $40,000, the break-even sales volume can be determined as follows:

$$\text{Break-Even Sales Units} = \frac{\$40,000}{(\$50 - \$30)}$$

$$\text{Break-Even Sales Units} = \frac{\$40,000}{\$20}$$

$$\text{Break-Even Sales Units} = 2,000 \text{ units}$$

Key Performance Indicators

In addition to high-level financial statement analysis, horizontal analysis, vertical analysis, and ratio analysis, a business should also consider using Key Performance Indicators (KPIs). These indicators may or may not use financial information from a financial statement. I know what you're thinking. This chapter is devoted to understanding financial statements so why would we even go down another path that has nothing to do with financial statements? Well, because it may be exactly the break-through your business needs to succeed. And I'm here to help in any way I can.

Financial statements are prepared after the fact; that is, after the operations occur. Net profit margin is a good ratio to measure, but it's a lagging indicator. Economists developed leading indicators to forecast the performance of the economy and coincident indicators to interpret the current status of the economy. Similarly, key performance indicators can be used by business owners to provide a sense of direction the business is headed in. [8]

Do you remember Continental Airlines? This company filed for Chapter 7 bankruptcy twice in the decade of the 1980s. The culture of the airline had been to drive down the costs per available seat mile, which is the standard cost measure in the airline industry. It cut costs at every opportunity by packing the planes with more seats, reducing food and drink portions, and paying its people poorly.

Gordon Bethune then took the helm as COO and President and began tracking three leading key performance indicators, including on-time arrival, lost luggage, and customer complaints. Continental Airlines had ranked dead last in these three categories. Key performance indicators measure success the same way the customer does. Every employee can influence the outcome of each such indicator, from the baggage handlers and flight crews to the gate agents and reservation operators.

Businesses fail because they want the right things but measure the wrong things or they measure the right things in the wrong way so they get the wrong results. Business owners need to define success the way their customers define it. Mr. Bethune understood the history of Continental Airlines' culture and said, "We aren't in business to save money, we are in business to put out a good product. You can make a pizza so cheap nobody wants to eat it. And you can make an airline so cheap nobody wants to fly it." [9]

Bethune then proceeded to turn the airline around between 1994 and 1997. Continental Airlines won more J.D. Power and Associates awards for Customer Satisfaction than any other airline in the world. *BusinessWeek* magazine named Bethune one of the top 25 Global Managers in 1996 and 1997. *Fortune* magazine ranked Continental Airlines the No. 1 Most Admired Global Airline in 2004 – 2008.

You can do the same for your business. Consider the following key performance indicators for your business. Don't implement them all; otherwise, you'll be overwhelmed with information overload and will know nothing about your business. Only adopt between three and seven that especially apply to your business.

Velocity KPIs

- Turnaround time – Tracking when each project comes in, establishing a desired completion date, and measuring the percentage of on-time delivery.
- Completed jobs/uncompleted jobs ratio – Each team member knows how many projects he or she is responsible for and the ratio of completion is tracked to project capacity into the future. [10]

Financial KPIs

- Revenue per person – Gross revenue divided by the number of full-time equivalent team members in the company; this result is then benchmarked against other companies to see how the business compares to the competition.
- Labor as a percentage of gross revenue – A useful metric for benchmarking against the competition.
- Innovation sales – Measures revenue from services introduced in recent years as well as the firm's innovation in offering additional services. Hewlett-Packard, for example, wants 50% of its revenue from products that did not exist two years ago.
- Net income % and profit per owner – These ratios provide an indication of whether the business is making adequate investments in its intellectual capital for the future or consuming all its profits in owner draws and wages. [11]

Pricing KPIs

- Percentage of proposals rejected – Tracks the company's success rate in getting customers to enter into long-term relationships with the company.
- Average difference between initial and final price – Provides a measure of whether the business is adequately qualifying the customer or determining exactly what the customer needs; it may also indicate that the business is not getting enough customer involvement into the design and terms of its proposals.
- Percentage of "reservation", "hope-for," and "pump-fist" price realized – A reservation price is the selling price at which a company will not accept below such price. A hope-for price is a selling price that will generate a *supernormal profit* for a company. A pump-fist price is the selling price that will generate a *windfall profit* for a company. Too high a percentage of pump-fist price realization could indicate that it is being set too low to begin with. Pump-fist realization should be between 20% and 40%, hope-for realization should be around 50%, and reservation realization should be 10% to 20%. [12]

Customer KPIs

- Customer loyalty – This metric must become part of the company's value system. After all, it costs an average of four to 11 times more to acquire a customer than to retain one.
- Share of customer wallet – This metric measures how well the business increasingly obtains new revenue from existing customers.
- Value gap – Measures how much revenue a business can potentially gain from a customer compared to how much revenue it actually gains.
- Percentage of Revenue from A, B, C, D, and F customers – Using airline terms, measures the amount of resources allocated between first-class, business-class, full-fare coach, coach, and bereavement fare passengers, respectively.
- Customer churn – Measures the number of customers lost compared to the number of customers gained.

- Forced churn – This metric helps a business abandon its C, D, and F customers by forcing it to fire between one and four such customers for every A and B customer acquired. [13]

Team-Member KPIs

- Marginal contribution to revenue – Measures the marginal contribution team members make to the company's revenue.
- Customer feedback – Measures how well team members deliver outstanding customer service.
- Innovation/creativity – Measures how often team members take risks or innovate new ways of doing things for customers or for the business. 3M implemented the "15 Percent Rule," which encourages technical people to spend up to 15% of their time on projects of their own choosing and initiative.
- Listening skills – Provides an indication of whether a team member listens to customers or other team members. After all, people do not care how much you know until they know how much you care.
- Knowledge elicitation – Measures how well the business educates its team members so that they generate their own knowledge.
- Continuous learning – Measures whether team members are constantly enhancing their skills to become more effective professionals.
- Effective delegation – Measures how effective managers and supervisors are at delegating to less experienced team members. It is estimated that 50% of the work done by managers and supervisors can be done by a more junior person.
- Mentoring and coaching – Measures how well the business develops team members who can coach and mentor less experienced team members.
- Personal development – Measures how effective the business is at inspiring and developing team members and helping them reach their personal goals.
- Personal marketing plan – Assists team members to follow through with their goals to arrange customer meetings and lunches, join professional organizations, giving speeches or seminars, writing articles, or cross-selling services.
- Number of customer contacts per week – Measures the effectiveness of team members in meeting regularly with customers they serve. [14]

Of course, there are industry-specific KPIs that a business might find appropriate to implement in addition to some of the above. For example, airlines might implement on-time arrival, lost luggage, and customer complaints as mentioned earlier. Restaurants might implement average daily seat turnover, average customer check, and customer counts. Accounting firms might implement turnaround time, monthly revenue trends, and client churn.

Evaluating the Quality of Financial Statements

Over the years, I've received telephone calls from frantic people telling me their business needs an audit. Sometimes it was because there has been a change in officers of a Home Owners

Association and the new officers suspect misappropriations of cash by the former officers. At other times it was because a group of potential new investors wanted to become comfortable that the financial statements were correct before making their investment. Often, however, after a brief explanation of what a financial statement audit entails and at what price, they realized that they really needed something lesser in scope.

Financial Statement Audits

Audits of financial statements are often required by financial institutions lending funds to their business customers and by shareholders of small- and medium-size corporations. Financial statement audits are also required by the Securities and Exchange Commission for public companies. Only CPAs are allowed to perform audits of financial statements.

An audit includes procedures to examine the evidence supporting the amounts and disclosures in the financial statements. After the audit work is complete, the CPA firm issues an audit report accompanying the audited financial statements which describes the nature of the examination and the CPA's opinion on the fairness of the financial statements.

The CPA firm does not guarantee absolute accuracy of financial statements nor does it guarantee that fraud was detected. However, the audit provides reasonable assurance to the users of the financial statements that the financial statements are free of material misstatement and fairly presented in accordance with accounting principles generally accepted in the United States. [15]

Quite a bit of planning must be done before the audit work begins. Also, the audit procedures themselves can be extensive and time-consuming. There is also much work to be done after the audit is substantially complete, including work to ensure that any loose ends are addressed, checklists are completed, and assistance with drafting the financial statements and notes to the financial statements is provided. In my experience, financial statement audit services can be priced between $10,000 and $100,000 for small- and medium-size businesses. However, the money is well-spent if it results in a large loan from a financial institution or an equity infusion by a group of investors. Also, as mentioned earlier, the IRS allows companies having audited financial statements to expense fixed assets costing less than $5,000.

Financial Statement Reviews

Your Aunt Betty may do a great job reconciling her bank statements and organizing her grocery receipts at her kitchen table, but she can't perform a review of your company's financial statements. Only CPAs are authorized to review financial statements and a review involves more than it sounds. Reviews of financial statements are often required by financial institutions lending funds to their business customers and by shareholders of small- and medium-size corporations. However, the amount of the loan or equity investment is relatively small and, therefore, the level of assurance required is also less than required for an audit.

A review includes analyzing trends and ratios, asking questions to understand the business, and other procedures. After the review work is complete, the CPA firm issues a review report accompanying the reviewed financial statements. A review report describes the nature of the examination and the CPA's opinion on whether there are any material modifications that should be made to the financial statements in order for them to be in conformity with accounting principles generally accepted in the United States or, if applicable, with any other comprehensive basis of accounting. [16]

Some planning must be done before the review work begins. Additionally, the review procedures and the related documentation take time, but less time than audit procedures. There is also work to be done after the review is substantially complete, including work to ensure that checklists are completed and assistance with drafting the financial statements and notes to the financial statements is provided. In my experience, financial statement review services can be priced between $5,000 and $15,000 for small- and medium-size businesses.

Financial Statement Compilations

Compilations of financial statements are often requested by small businesses without accounting personnel or with accounting personnel with limited accounting experience and education. These services can be performed monthly, quarterly, semi-annually, or annually.

When performing compilation services, the accounting firm reviews the company's general ledger, proposes correcting journal entries, and then "compiles" or prepares financial statements so that the owners and managers can evaluate the financial performance of their business. After the compilation work is complete, the accounting firm issues a compilation report accompanying the compiled financial statements, but does not provide any assurance regarding the accuracy of the financial statements. [17]

Agreed-Upon Procedures

Agreed-upon procedures are often requested by small- and medium-size businesses and have been discussed and agreed to by the company's management and the accounting firm. The procedures are limited in scope and are intended to provide specific information for management to make decisions about the business, but do not provide any assurance regarding the sufficiency of the procedures. For example, the new officers of a Home Owners Association who suspect that cash may have been misappropriated by the former officers may, instead of a full-blown financial statement audit, request agreed-upon procedures such as a proof of cash to determine whether funds were actually misappropriated.

In the next chapter, we'll discuss converting your income statement into a cash flow statement so that you can determine where your company's cash is coming from and where it's going.

8 – Preparing Cash Flow Statements

In Chapter 3, I mentioned that cash does not necessarily represent net profit. We discussed loan proceeds that are not income and loan payments that are not expenses since loan proceeds and repayments simply change loan payable balances on the balance sheet. Also when a company reports on the accrual basis, it recognizes income when it bills the customer but does not yet collect cash. A company can purchase equipment by financing it and, therefore, doesn't pay cash at the time of purchase.

The balance sheet and the income statement that we've previously studied do not directly reflect the cash flow of the business. However, business owners are very concerned about where their cash is coming from and where it's going. This is where the Cash Flow Statement comes in. It provides information about cash received and paid out during a particular period of time and provides information about financing and investing activities during the period.

In this chapter, we'll discuss the different sections of the cash flow statement and the step-by-step instructions on how to prepare the statement.

Cash Flow Statement Components

A Cash Flow Statement is divided into three main sections, including Net Cash Flow from Operating Activities, Cash Flows from Investing Activities, and Cash Flows from Financing Activities.

Net Cash Flow from Operating Activities

Routine business operations are probably a business's most important source of cash since normal profit-directed activities provide the cash needed by the company. Therefore, it's logical that this section is presented first in the Cash Flow Statement.

Operating activities include events and transactions associated with the sale of goods and services to customers. Accordingly, the cash received from customers are included in cash inflows from operating activities. Cash payments to suppliers for goods purchased and salary and wage payments to employees are included in cash outflows from operating activities.

We can directly analyze a business's operating transactions to determine the effect of operations on the cash balance. However, it is usually easier to begin with net income and then make adjustments to determine the cash generated from operating activities. Net income is adjusted to net cash flow from operating activities for the following:

- Amounts included in net income that do not affect the business's cash flow.
- Changes in current asset and current liability account balances.
- Gains or losses on the sale of noncurrent assets (fixed assets, e.g.).

Examples of amounts included in net income that do not affect cash flow are depreciation and amortization. These expenses are recorded over the useful lives of the assets, but cash is not actually paid out.

Examples of changes in current asset and current liability account balances are accounts receivable, inventory, accounts payable, and accrued liabilities. Under the accrual basis of accounting, these balances reflect the recognition of revenue or expenses in a different period than when the cash is collected or paid, respectively.

The effects of gains or losses on the sale of noncurrent assets must also be removed from net cash flow from operating activities, because the cash proceeds must be shown under Cash Flows from Investing Activities instead. Gains must be subtracted from and losses must be added to net income to arrive at cash flow from operating activities. [18]

Cash Flows from Investing Activities

Cash flows from investing activities result from the purchase or sale of noncurrent assets, lending money, or the collection of loans. For example, when long-term investments, fixed assets, or other noncurrent assets are purchased outright (rather than financed), cash is reduced by the amount paid. When long-term investments, fixed assets, or other noncurrent assets are sold, cash is increased by the amount received. If a business makes a loan, cash is decreased by the amount of cash paid and when a business collects principal payments on a loan, cash increases. [19]

Cash Flows from Financing Activities

Cash flows from financing activities result from the issuance or repurchase of company stock, the proceeds from or repayment of debt, and the payment of dividends or distributions. For example, when a corporation issues common stock, cash increases by the amount of cash received by the company from the investor and when a corporation reacquires its own common stock as treasury stock, cash is reduced by the amount of cash paid to redeem it. Incurring a loan from a bank increases cash by the amount of cash received. When payments are made to reduce the debt, cash is decreased by the amount of the repayment. When a corporation pays a cash dividend or a cash distribution to a shareholder, cash is decreased. [20]

Be aware that in a formal Cash Flow Statement, certain financing and investing activities that did not actually affect cash must be disclosed, but is beyond the scope of this book.

Steps to Prepare a Cash Flow Statement

Step 1 – Begin with Final Financial Statements

A cash flow statement uses the ending balance sheet and income statement balances. Therefore, make sure that your financial statements have been reviewed by the appropriate managers or business owners and that all adjusting and correcting journal entries have been recorded, and that they are final. They should also be final before attempting to analyze and interpret financial statements, but it's especially common for an eager beaver to begin preparing a cash flow statement before all the balances have been finalized. If corrections are made to the balance sheet or to the income statement after the cash flow statement has begun to be prepared, it has to be prepared again from the beginning.

Step 2 – Calculate the Change in Balance Sheet Balances

Determine the difference between the ending balances and beginning balances of each of the balance sheet amounts by referencing the Balance Sheet.

Step 3 – Determine Specific Changes in Specific Balance Sheet Balances

For certain asset, liability, and equity balances, more specific detail must be obtained to account for the changes during the period. For example, consider the following:

- Investments – Cash paid for purchases, net amount disposed, unrealized gain or loss, cash received for sales, realized gain or loss on sales, and any noncash transactions.
- Accounts Receivable – Bad debt expense and other increases or decreases.
- Employee Advances – Cash paid for new loans to and cash received for loan repayments from employees.
- Fixed Assets – Depreciation expense, cash paid for purchases, net amount disposed, cash received for sales, and realized gain or loss on sales.
- Intangible Assets – Amortization expense, cash paid for purchases, net amount disposed, cash received for sales, and realized gain or loss on sales.
- Notes Receivable – Cash paid for new loans provided and cash received for loan repayments received.
- Loans from Owners – Cash received for new loans provided by and cash paid for loan repayments to owners.
- Capital Lease Obligations - Cash paid for capital lease obligation repayments to leasing companies.
- Lines of Credit (LOC) – Cash received for new line of credit loan proceeds from and cash paid for line of credit repayments to lenders.
- Notes Payable - Cash received for new term loan proceeds from and cash paid for term loan repayments to lenders.
- Equity – Cash dividends or cash distributions paid to investors, net income or loss, cash paid to repurchase stock, cash received from stock issued to investors, and any noncash transactions.

Step 4 – Identify Revenue and Expenses

Identify total amounts in the broad categories of sales revenue, interest and dividend income, gain or loss on disposal or sale of assets, miscellaneous income, cost of sales, payroll expenses, interest expense, income taxes, and other operating expenses.

Step 5 – Complete the Net Cash Flow from Operating Activities Section

The following worksheet may be used to complete the Net Cash Flow from Operating Activities section of the Cash Flow Statement with information obtained in steps 1 – 4 above. Note that the words in brackets indicate that an amount should be treated as a deduction.

Net Income (Loss)	
Adjustments:	
Depreciation and Amortization	
(Gain) Loss on Disposal of Investments	
(Gain) Loss on Disposal of Assets	
Bad Debt Expense	
Unrealized (Gain) Loss on Investments	
(Increase) Decrease in Assets:	
Accounts Receivable, net	
Interest Receivable	
Due from Owners	
Employee Advances	
Prepaid Expenses	
Inventory	
Deposits	
Other Assets	
Increase (Decrease) in Liabilities:	
Accounts Payable	
Accrued Payroll	
Accrued Interest Payable	
Accrued Payroll Taxes	
Accrued Sales Taxes	
Accrued Income Taxes	
Other Accrued Liabilities	
Cash Provided (Used) by Operating Activities	

Step 6 – Complete the Cash Flows from Investing Activities Section

The following worksheet may be used to complete the Cash Flows from Investing Activities section of the Cash Flow Statement with information obtained in steps 1 – 4 above. Note that the words in brackets indicate that an amount should be treated as a deduction.

(Purchases) of Investments	
Proceeds from Sale of Investments	
(Purchases) of Fixed Assets	
Proceeds from Sale of Fixed Assets	
(Issuance) of Notes Receivable	
Repayments on Notes Receivable	
Cash Provided (Used) by Investing Activities	

Step 7 – Complete the Cash Flows from Financing Activities Section

The following worksheet may be used to complete the Cash Flows from Financing Activities section of the Cash Flow Statement with information obtained in steps 1 – 4 above. Note that the words in brackets indicate that an amount should be treated as a deduction.

Borrowing from Owners	
(Repayments) of Loans to Owners	
Proceeds from Debt	
(Repayments) of Debt	
(Repayments) of Capital Lease Obligations	
Net Borrowing on (Repayments of) LOC	
(Dividends/Distributions) to Owners	
(Repurchase) of Stock	
Capital Contributions by Owners	
Cash Provided (Used) by Financing Activities	

Step 8 – Complete the Cash Rollforward Section

The following worksheet may be used to complete the "Cash Rollforward" section of the Cash Flow Statement with information obtained in steps 1 – 4 above. Note that the words in brackets indicate that an amount should be treated as a deduction.

Net Increase (Decrease) in Cash (sum of cash flow in each of the three sections)	
Cash at Beginning of Period (must agree to cash balance per the prior period Balance Sheet)	
Cash at End of Period (must agree to cash balance per the current period Balance Sheet)	

The amounts per the above worksheets may be transferred to a formal Statement of Cash Flows included as part of the business's financial statements. Note that the resulting Cash

Flow Statement was prepared using the Indirect Method, which is used by most businesses that prepare cash flow statements.

A Cash Flow Statement may also, however, be prepared using the Direct Method, which may be easier for the business owners to understand. While there is no difference between the Cash Flows from Investing Activities and Cash Flows from Financing Activities using either method, the Net Cash Flow from Operating Activities is presented in a more useful manner.

While beyond the scope of this book, the Net Cash Flow from Operating Activities section prepared using the Direct Method presents the following information rather than a reconciliation of net income to cash provided or used by operating activities:

> Cash Collected from Customers
> Interest Received
> Cash Paid to Suppliers
> Cash Paid to Employees and Owners
> Interest Paid
> Income Taxes Paid

Appendix C includes information about Microsoft Excel-based worksheet files to assist you in preparing a Cash Flow Statement for your business using either the Indirect Method or Direct Method.

In the next chapter, we'll discuss how to prepare budgets and cash forecasts so you'll have additional tools to more effectively run your business.

9 – Preparing Budgets and Cash Forecasts

In this chapter, we'll discuss the purpose of a budget and the steps necessary to prepare both annual and monthly budgets based on the income statement and annual and monthly cash forecasts based on the budgets.

What Exactly is a Budget?

What does the word "budget" sound like to you? Homework? I admit, no one really likes to prepare a budget. Well, except engineers. A budget allows you to tell your money where to go (not vice versa). A budget gives you control over your business finances. A budget is an operating plan that allows you to compare your budgeted sales and expenses to actual sales and expenses every month. Overall operating budgets are frequently called projected financial statements and the starting point for developing a budget is the historical income statements. [1]

We said earlier that financial statements will help you adjust your marketing efforts quickly so that you may react and regain control over your spending, but a budget will give you a turbo boost with this. You will be able to clearly see the variations from budgeted amounts, which will be alarm signals to adjust quickly.

I know what you're thinking. I see you sitting back in your easy chair with Fluffy on your lap and a cold one in your hand. I smell the frozen pizza baking in the oven. I hear you scoffing, "Ehh! I don't need a budget! I've doing just fine without one."

What can happen if you don't have a budget for your business? Well, you can easily go out of business. For example, if your company has $100,000 on hand at the start of the year and by the end of the year your company has cash sales of $500,000 but cash expenditures of $800,000, then there is a $200,000 cash shortage. The only way to make sure that you have enough sales to cover your expenses is to create a budget and abide by it.

Zig Ziglar said, "If you aim at nothing, you will hit it every time." [2] If you want to save a lot of money in very little time, create a budget. Dave Ramsey of Financial Peace University says that money is active. That's why it's called "currency." Money flows from businesses that don't manage it well to those that do.

An effective budgeting system involves both planning and control. The fact that budgeting forces business owners and managers to plan is important. When preparing a budget, the owners and managers have to turn away from daily operations and think about their goals. Planning involves setting goals and developing strategies to meet them.

Control involves determining whether objectives are being achieved by comparing actual results to planned results and taking appropriate corrective actions. [3]

Steps to Prepare a Budget

Step 1 – Dream a Little

Yes, you read that correctly. I see you chuckling and almost choking on your deluxe pizza with mild Italian sausage, pepperoni, ground beef, black olives, and onions. Business owners as well as managers who are responsible for the revenue-generating department should start with their dreams. Not dreams for their business or department just yet, but personal dreams.

Think about your perfect day away from the business. What do you do now that you really enjoy? What would you like to do more? What have you never done, but would like to do? Turn off your digital devices and close your eyes for a moment. Would you like to have a luxurious log cabin retirement home in the mountains? A vacation home at the beach overlooking emerald green water and white sand? Would you play more golf perhaps at an upscale country club? Travel to tour ancient castles in jolly old England?

These personal dreams will motivate you to begin developing dreams for your business or department. Now think about your perfect day at the business. What do you do now that you really enjoy? What would you like to do more? What have you never done, but would like to? If your business can grow 15% a year, it will double in five years. If it can grow 25% a year, it will double in only three years. Would you like to come in to the business only two or three days a week? Check in with managers and review their projects and progress? Call a loyal customer and take him or her to lunch? Check on other business ventures, real estate properties, and investments? Surpass a sales goal? Make a lot of money?

These personal and business dreams will motivate you to begin defining your goals.

Step 2 – Define Your Goals

Business owners and managers should next take some time and define both their financial and non-financial goals. Most business owners' ideal businesses involve the following:

- Three or four weeks off every year to travel.
- A business run by a trusted management team empowered to make decisions and get things done.
- A unique and excellent product or service which allows them to charge more than their competitors.
- Business systems in place that produce consistent results for their customers and improves their net profits year after year.
- 90% of their business coming from loyal repeat customers *who only buy from them*.
- 25% annual net return on their equity.
- A business that will allow them to expand, find additional business opportunities, and grow their net worth.
- Control of their future and time to enjoy the benefits of ownership.

Do a little brainstorming and list 20 or 30 goals and then rank them in order of priority. Next, classify them into short-, medium-, and long-term goals. Short-term goals are achievable within the next year. Medium-term goals are able to be accomplished between two and ten years. Long-term goals take more than ten years to fulfill. See Appendix D for tools to assist you in documenting, prioritizing, and tracking your goals.

Step 3 – Determine a Sales Goal

The next step in developing a budget is to put the dreams and goals into a financial plan to help you achieve those dreams and goals. We will assume that the budget period is for a year. The first part of an annual budget and the driving force is annual budgeted sales. Great care should be given to the preparation of budgeted sales, because it is the basis for budgeting cost of sales and operating expenses. Budgeted sales is simply a realistic estimate of the number of units of product or services to be sold at each product's and service's unit sales price during the year. The sales trend in recent years should be considered along with economic conditions, expected industry developments, and market research. [4]

I know the temptation. You're thinking, "Yeah, baby! We can increase sales by 50% over last year!" However, if your estimated increase in sales is not realistic, you'll be disappointed month after month when your business isn't close to achieving the budgeted sales goal. Then you'll lose interest is obtaining your goals, you'll start coming in later and later each day, you'll stop wearing business dress or business casual dress in favor of board shorts and Hawaiian shirts, you'll decide to stop at the local bar on your way to the company and not even come in, and eventually find yourself unable to pay your mortgage, and end up sitting on a curb with a tin cup in your hand begging for money. Don't let this happen to you all because you wildly overestimated your budgeted sales.

Step 4 – Determine Expenses Goals

Once budgeted sales is determined, budgeted materials cost of sales can be developed, if applicable. The business must have enough inventory during the year to meet product sales demand and also have enough inventory on hand at the end of the year to meet immediate demand in the first part of the following year. Therefore, the estimated cost of sales is a function of the number of units projected to be sold and the number of units desired at the end of the year. The total is the quantity needed during the year. The number of inventory units on hand at the beginning of the year is then subtracted from this quantity to determine the number of units to be produced or purchased during the year. [5]

If the business has established a consistent and efficient materials cost of sales as a percentage of sales, that percentage may be used as a starting point for estimated cost of sales. Of course, if you can reduce the cost from the previous year by changing vendors, for example, while maintaining the same quality, that would be optimal.

Estimated direct labor is the estimated number of direct labor hours expected to be worked at average labor cost per hour during the year. Again, this is directly related to the expected sales for the year. [6]

Now let's look at operating expenses. The prior year amounts may be used as a starting point, but every expense line item should be challenged. If possible, you should compare what your business is spending to what your competitors are spending to make sure you're getting the best deals. I imagine that some of you may be asking how you can know what your competitors are spending. Well, there are industry reports available from various sources at a price. See Appendix E for an additional resource to help you uncover the expenses of your competitors. Also, when challenging each line item, consider how you might reduce the cost in the budget.

In developing your budget, consider the following selected operating expenses:

- Advertising – According to a ComScore research study, less than 20% of advertising campaigns by U.S. companies (with marketing budgets between $400,000 and $2,000,000) reached their target audience. Therefore, you must know who your target audience is. Understand the way they think, the way they talk, their beliefs and opinions, how they spend their free time, and what they read. Then place targeted ads with strong offers, differentiation factors, and benefits of your company. Then test your ads' different headlines, offers, publications, and geographic locations. Finally, measure the results and focus on the ads that really work. You should spend at least the same percentage of sales as your competitors in advertising.
- Amortization – Simply use the depreciation schedule from you accountant in budgeting for this expense. Most income tax software includes schedules for the current tax year as well as the next tax year.
- Automobile Expenses – If your business uses an accountable plan, make sure you enforce its use and require employees to submit reimbursement requests for business travel each month.
- Credit Card Fees – Obtain bids from at least three credit card merchant service companies and make sure you're getting the lowest possible fees for the credit cards you accept.
- Depreciation – Again, simply use the depreciation schedule from you accountant in budgeting for this expense. Most income tax software includes schedules for the current tax year as well as the next tax year. If you anticipate significant new purchases of equipment, furniture, or facilities, ask your accountant to assist you in estimating additional depreciation expense for the year.
- Dues and Subscriptions – Does your office lobby really need 20 different magazine subscriptions for your customers while they wait? They're probably just checking their social media on their devices anyway.
- Insurance – Obtain bids from at least three insurance companies each year and make sure you're getting the lowest possible premium at the desired level of coverage.

- Leases – Automobiles – If it makes sense for your business to have an automobile primarily for business use, have the business buy a pre-owned car instead of leasing. What? Sophisticated people lease cars! *Smart Money* magazine has told us that leasing a car is the worst possible way to acquire a vehicle. After all, the effective interest rate is 14%!
- Marketing – When you're paying for marketing, you may feel like it's an expense. However, when done properly, it's an investment. If you spend $1,000 on a marketing campaign that generates $2,000 in income in two weeks, then you double your money. Now that's a good investment.
- Meals and Entertainment – The business should only be paying for meals and entertainment when there is an opportunity to generate new business from it. Establish clear guidelines for your team members when incurring such expenses. Some meals, however, are necessary "for the employer's convenience" when team members attend all-day seminars or are working out of town.
- Miscellaneous – This exposes the accountant in me, but this expense line item should be budgeted at zero. Every expense should have a specific category other than "miscellaneous" or "other."
- Rent – The industry average rent as a percentage of sales is a very helpful indicator of what your business should be paying in rent. If you're paying significantly more, you should seriously look to relocate.
- Repairs and Maintenance – As equipment and buildings age, it's natural for their repair costs to increase. However, at some point, you're spending too much in repairs and it may be time to replace with new property.
- Royalty Fees – Royalty fees are usually a specified percentage of sales as defined in a franchised business's franchise agreement.
- Taxes – Payroll – Payroll taxes may be estimated as a percentage of estimated salaries and wages. Remember, this expense line item includes only the employer's share of FICA taxes and state and federal unemployment taxes.
- Taxes – Property – Property taxes may be estimated based on annual assessments for the budget year or simply based on the prior year amounts paid if the values haven't changed significantly.
- Travel – Search internet sites that provide nightly prices for all hotels and motels in the area to ensure you're getting the best value for the money. Yes, this can be done for business, too. Also consider bidding for high-end lodgings. You never know what kind of great deal you might get.
- Gain/Loss on Disposal of Assets – If you know you're going to sell or dispose of fixed assets, go ahead and plan for the gain or loss (and also reduce depreciation expense for the depreciation not to be claimed after the disposal).

Step 5 – Review and Finalize the Annual Budget

When the budgeted sales and expenses have been documented, review the budget for reasonableness. Also have everyone involved in the process review the budget and make any changes deemed necessary. Make sure you've budgeted for a desirable net profit for the year.

If budgeted sales less budgeted expenses results in a budgeted net loss for the year, you might need to make some corrections.

Step 6 – Create Monthly Budgets from the Annual Budget

When everyone is satisfied with the annual budget, divide the annual amounts among the months in the year. Use the following as a guide:

- Sales – Budgeted sales may be determined for each month by referencing the prior year monthly financial statements. Sales tend to follow certain trends for most businesses so it wouldn't make sense to simply divide the annual amount by 12 and allocate evenly to each month. For example, ice cream shops sell more ice cream and soft drinks in the warm summer months. Accounting firms sell most of their income tax services during the tax filing season. Just make sure the total of the budgeted monthly sales equals the budgeted annual sales after they're allocated.
- Cost of Sales – Materials cost of sales in the annual budget may already be a fixed percentage of sales. If so, that percentage can simply be multiplied by the budgeted monthly sales to determine the budgeted monthly materials cost of sales. If cost of sales is a function of the estimated number of units to be sold at an estimated cost per unit or some other methodology, determine budgeted monthly materials cost of sales in that manner.
- Direct Labor – Budgeted monthly direct labor should be a function of the estimated monthly sales.
- Salaries and Wages – Budgeted annual salaries and wages may be allocated evenly to each month for simplicity. However, if your business is seasonal and you hire many temporary employees during seasonal periods, be sure to account for the increased wages. If salaries and wages are paid weekly, you might wish to determined which two months during the year include five weeks rather than four weeks and add a little precision to the estimated monthly amounts.
- Advertising – Budgeted monthly advertising should probably be a function of the estimated monthly sales.
- Credit Card Fees – Based on the credit cards accepted by the business, budgeted monthly credit card fees should be an average of the credit card fees as a percentage of monthly estimated sales.
- Insurance – If premiums are paid monthly, budgeted annual insurance can simply be allocated evenly to each month. However, if premiums are paid at one time for several months of coverage and your business is on the cash basis of accounting, the budgeted amounts should be allocated to the specific months when the premiums are expected to be paid.
- Security Monitoring Fees – Budgeted security monitoring fees should be allocated to the months in which they are expected to be paid. Some fees are paid every month while other fees are paid quarterly, for example.
- Taxes – Payroll – Budgeted monthly payroll taxes should be a fixed percentage of estimated monthly salaries and wages.

- Taxes – Property – Budgeted property taxes should be allocated to the months in which they are expected to be paid. Most municipalities and county governments bill property taxes in September through December each year.
- Utilities – While not usually significant in amount, utilities vary each month depending on the weather. Therefore, monthly budgeted utilities may be estimated by reference to the prior year monthly financial statements.

Most other budgeted monthly expenses not identified above may simply be allocated evenly to each month. However, please use your judgment. After everyone involved reviews and agrees to the monthly budget amounts, the amounts may be input into the accounting software so that budgeted income statements may be prepared along with the actual income statements in the budget year. Budgeted income statements, again, present actual amounts compared to budgeted amounts and also present a dollar amount variance and a percentage variance from the budgeted amounts.

Tips for Developing a Budget

All right, enough already with budgets! One more thing. The following tips might be helpful when developing your budget:

- Plan to work on the budget in several sessions during one week.
- Work out the budget with everyone who will be affected by it and who have responsibility for it.
- Be realistic and specific to your business.
- Refer to your financial goals when setting priorities.
- Use round numbers, if possible.

Steps to Prepare a Cash Forecast

Let's review. Net income or loss per the income statement does not necessarily equal the cash balance in the bank account. A budget is based on historical income statements and, accordingly, does not budget for cash inflows and outflows. This is where a cash forecast comes in. Don't worry. A cash forecast is simply an adaptation of the annual and monthly budgets. Cash is king for any business, right? A cash forecast will help your business save cash by spending only on planned expenditures.

Step 1 – Start with the Beginning Reconciled Cash Balance

Document your beginning cash balance from the bank reconciliation that was prepared. Easy.

Step 2 – Identify Cash Inflows

By referencing the budgeted sales, adjust for any sales not expected to be collected by customers in the year and then document the expected cash sales. Then add any expected collections on accounts receivable from the prior year. Next, determine any proceeds expected from loans. Determine any sale proceeds expected from sales of assets. Estimated any investment income. Finally, estimate any capital contributions from owners.

Step 2 – Identify Cash Outflows

Again, by referencing the budgeted expenses, adjust for any expenditures not expected to be paid to vendors during the year and document the expected cash purchases of materials, inventory, and operating expenses. Then add any expected payments on accounts payable from the prior year. Next, determine payment of cash salaries and wages to be paid. This may be taken directly from the budget if the company doesn't normally accrue salaries and wages at the end of each year. Determine any expected repayments of loans. Determine any expected purchases of fixed assets. Don't forget to estimate payments for income taxes if the business is a regular C Corporation. Finally, estimate any dividends or distributions to owners. Note that amortization and depreciation expenses from the budget are not used in a cash forecast, because they're not actually cash payments.

Step 3 – Complete the Annual Cash Forecast Worksheet

The following worksheet may be used in preparing your annual cash forecast. You can include as much detail for expenditures as in the budget. In my opinion, the more detail, the more information you'll have in order to determine any spending corrections to be made during the year.

Beginning Cash Balance	
ADD: Cash Receipts	
Cash Sales	
Collections on Receivables	
Loan Proceeds Received	
Sale Proceeds from Asset Sales	
Investment Income	
Owner Capital Contributions	
Total Cash Inflows	
DEDUCT: Cash Disbursements	
Cash Materials and Inventory Purchases	
Cash Operating Costs	
Payment of Payables	
Loan Repayments	
Purchase of Fixed Assets	
Income Taxes	
Owner Dividends or Distributions	
Total Cash Outflows	
Ending Cash Balance	

Step 4 – Create Monthly Cash Forecasts from the Annual Cash Forecast

After the annual forecast is completed, divide the annual amounts among the months in the year using the allocations in the monthly budgets as a guide.

In the next chapter, we'll provide some tips on selecting an accountant for your business.

10 – How to Choose an Accountant

Well that was a lot of information in just a few pages. If you've read the entire book, you learned about each of the balance sheet and income statement accounts, you understand debits and credits, you know the difference between the cash and accrual basis of accounting, you learned how to record transactions and close the books, you can now analyze your financial statements in order to improve your business, and can even prepare cash flow statements and budgets.

I'll ask again. Are you sure you want to spend your valuable time, or your team members' valuable time, struggling with the accounting? I know the accounting is very exciting and each transaction is as new and fresh as a tulip blossoming in the spring, but wouldn't you rather be on the golf course making a sale or taking a customer to lunch? I know from personal experience the satisfaction one gains from a balanced journal entry, but wouldn't it be just as satisfying to begin choosing architect drawings for that new French Polynesian bungalow in Tahiti?

Yes, of course you would. I knew that if I made the accounting process seem intimidating enough, you'd eventually see it in a new light. You've made an excellent decision and I know you won't regret it. In all seriousness, regardless of the extent your business is involved in the day-to-day accounting, you'll most likely need an accountant at some point.

First of all, I recommend that you choose a CPA firm over a bookkeeping firm or a non-CPA accounting firm. CPAs are highly educated and they must have a bachelor's degree in accounting. They must obtain 40 hours of continuing professional education each year in order to remain current with frequently changing tax laws and accounting standards. CPAs are experienced and, before being granted their CPA certificate, they must have at least two years of experience with a public accounting firm or at least five years of experience working under a CPA in a private company. CPAs have credentials. To become licensed, they must pass the CPA exam, which is one of the most rigorous exams in all professions. CPAs are also trustworthy. Most CPAs are members of the AICPA or state CPA organizations who must abide by a strict code of ethics and whose firms must undergo a quality review once every three years.

Second, I recommend that you look for the following when making a decision about a CPA firm:

- Ensure that the professional is a good listener. Ask them for an introductory meeting, which should be complimentary, and then assess whether they do all the talking rather than asking questions and listening to you.
- Ensure that the firm is proactive. Determine whether it sends newsletters that do more than regurgitate proposed or passed tax legislation. Good newsletters should provide true value and help your business or help you personally improve.

- Ensure that the firm members have great experience. Professionals who have worked with large local, national, or international CPA firms typically have seen a variety of complex issues and will be very competent. Likewise, professionals who have worked in management positions with Fortune 500 companies also have excellent backgrounds.
- Ensure that the firm has special experience with your business's industry. Ask them if they have such a niche. If your business is a franchised business, a dental practice, or a construction company, for example, you have unique accounting and reporting issues that are very different from generic service-based businesses.
- Ensure that the firm's billing rates are reasonable. There certainly is a trust factor that develops after working with a particular firm over time, but it is amazing to me that some people never shop around a bit just to see if what they're paying is worth the value received.
- Ensure that you're comfortable with the firm's fee structure. Inquire whether the firm typically charges by the hour or at fixed fees. Fixed fees may help you avoid any surprises and will help you budget for the annual investment.
- Ensure that the firm provides added-value services. Most CPA firms help you comply with IRS tax return filing requirements, can help you reduce your income taxes with tax planning services, and can assist you in preparing financial statements for your business, but do they also help you think strategically about your business and partner with you on an advisory basis to improve your business?

Third, I recommend that you see Appendix F for more about the author of this book and Appendix G for his firm's contact information.

I'm certain that any reasonable fees that your business will pay to a quality professional CPA firm will pale in comparison to the benefits you'll receive. Similar to the concrete and steel foundation of a skyscraper office building, an effective accounting system is the foundation of any successful business. Once your financial statements can be relied upon in a timely manner, they will provide invaluable information about the past performance of your business, the current financial health of your business, and a basis for planning strategically for a successful future of your business!

Appendix A

Sample Chart of Accounts for a Corporation

Account Number	Account Description
1000	Cash
1001	Cash
1020	Petty Cash
1110	Accounts Receivable
1111	Allowance for Doubtful Accounts
1120	Due from Affiliates
1140	Due from Stockholders
1160	Employee Advances
1200	Inventory
1300	Prepaid Expenses
1310	Prepaid Insurance
1320	Prepaid Payroll
1330	Prepaid Payroll Taxes
1340	Prepaid Federal Income Taxes
1350	Prepaid State Income Taxes
1400	Investments
1410	Deferred Tax Benefit
1490	Other Current Assets
1500	Automobiles
1510	Buildings
1520	Equipment
1530	Furniture and Fixtures
1540	Land
1550	Leasehold Improvements
1560	Signs
1570	Software
1599	Accumulated Depreciation
1600	Customer List
1610	Franchise Fees
1620	Goodwill
1630	Loan Origination Costs
1640	Noncompetition Agreement
1650	Organization Costs
1660	Start-up Costs
1699	Accumulated Amortization
1700	Security Deposits
1710	Deferred Tax Benefit
1800	Investments
2000	Accounts Payable
2020	Due to Affiliates
2200	Accrued FICA Withholding

Account Number	Account Description
2205	Accrued Federal Withholding
2210	Accrued State Withholding
2220	Accrued State Unemployment Taxes
2230	Accrued Federal Unemployment Taxes
2240	Accrued Commissions
2250	Accrued Credit Card Liabilities
2260	Accrued Dividends
2270	Accrued Interest
2280	Accrued Retirement Plan Contributions
2290	Accrued Sales Taxes
2310	Deferred Tax Liability
2370	Accrued Federal Income Taxes
2380	Accrued State Income Taxes
2390	Customer Deposits
2399	Current Portion Long-term Debt
2400	Note Payable
2410	Note Payable
2440	Note Payable – Stockholders
2510	Deferred Tax Liability
3000	Common Stock
3010	Preferred Stock
3020	Additional Paid-in Capital
3030	Dividends – Cash
3031	Dividends – Property
3032	Dividends – Stock
3040	Treasury Stock
3050	Retained Earnings
3060	Unrealized Gain/Loss on Investments
4000	Sales
4090	Returns and Allowances
4999	Beginning Inventory
5000	Purchases
5010	Cost of Labor
5020	Freight and Delivery
5030	Supplies
5999	Ending Inventory
6000	Officer Salaries
6010	Salaries and Wages
6030	Advertising
6040	Amortization
6110	Automobile Expenses
6115	Bad Debts
6120	Bank Service Fees
6130	Cash Over/Short
6140	Charitable Contributions
6141	Commissions
6142	Communications
6143	Computer Expenses

Account Number	Account Description
6144	Contract Labor
6145	Consulting Fees
6147	Country Club Dues
6148	Credit Card Fees
6150	Depreciation
6160	Dues and Subscriptions
6170	Education and Training
6172	Employee Benefits
6175	Franchise Fees
6180	Insurance – Automobiles
6181	Insurance – Group Disability
6182	Insurance – Group Health
6183	Insurance – Liability
6184	Insurance – Officer Life
6185	Insurance – Professional Liability
6186	Insurance – Stockholders' Disability
6187	Insurance – Stockholders' Health
6190	Insurance – Workers' Compensation
6200	Interest
6205	Internet Service Fees
6206	Janitorial Fees
6207	Landscaping and Lawncare
6208	Laundry
6209	Leases – Automobiles
6210	Leases – Equipment
6220	Legal and Accounting Fees
6230	Licenses and Permits
6231	Management Fees
6232	Marketing
6233	Meals and Entertainment
6235	Medical Reimbursements
6236	Meetings
6240	Miscellaneous
6242	Music
6245	Office Supplies
6246	Parking and Tolls
6247	Payroll Processing Fees
6248	Penalties
6249	Political Contributions
6250	Postage and Delivery
6260	Printing and Reproduction
6270	Professional Fees
6280	Professional Gifts
6285	Recruiting Fees
6286	Reference Materials
6287	Relocation Fees
6290	Rent – Facilities
6300	Repairs and Maintenance

Account Number	Account Description
6310	Retirement Plan Administrative Fees
6320	Retirement Plan Contributions
6321	Royalty Fees
6322	Security
6323	Small Equipment
6324	Software
6325	Storage Fees
6326	Supplies
6327	Taxes – Payroll
6328	Taxes – Property
6329	Taxes – Other
6330	Telephone – Cellular
6340	Telephone – Land Line
6345	Temporary Help
6349	Training
6350	Travel
6380	Uniforms
6390	Utilities
6395	Waste Disposal
6810	Taxes – Federal Income
6820	Taxes – State Income
6830	Taxes – Local Income
7000	Gain/Loss on Disposal of Assets
7010	Interest Income
7020	Vendor's Compensation
7030	Other Income
7040	State Income Tax Refunds
7100	Ordinary Income/Loss from Passthroughs
7101	Net Rental Income/Loss from Passthroughs
7102	Guaranteed Payments from Passthroughs
7103	Interest Income from Passthroughs
7104	Dividend Income from Passthroughs
7105	Royalties from Passthroughs
7106	Short-term Capital Gain/Loss from Passthroughs
7107	Long-term Capital Gain/Loss from Passthroughs
7108	Net Section 1231 Gain/Loss from Passthroughs
7109	Other Income/Loss from Passthroughs
7110	Section 179 Deduction from Passthroughs
7111	Charitable Contributions from Passthroughs
7112	Other Deductions from Passthroughs
7113	Tax-exempt Income from Passthroughs
7114	Nondeductible Expenses from Passthroughs
7115	Section 754 Depreciation from Passthroughs
8010	Other Expenses
9999	Suspense

Appendix B

Financial Performance Review

Rather than crunching the numbers yourself in analyzing your business financial statements, let Allen & Company partner with you and help you understand what they're telling you. Using your annual financial statements, we can prepare a comprehensive, easy-to-understand report that assesses the financial health of your business and compares your business to similar businesses in your industry.

This Financial Performance Review highlights the areas of your business that are the strongest and those which need improvement. The report also provides several powerful tips that you can start implementing immediately to improve your business.

To obtain your Financial Performance Review, please send us your business annual financial statements or income tax returns for the previous two years and we'll get started.

www.allenandcompanypc.com

Appendix C

Cash Flow Statement Worksheets

Don't struggle with creating your cash flow statements. Use Allen & Company's Microsoft Excel worksheets to create your statements. While most accounting software can generate a Cash Flow Statement, the statement is usually limited to the indirect method, which isn't as meaningful as statements prepared using the direct method. Also, they usually don't agree to professionally-prepared cash flow statements, due to basic setup parameters. With Allen & Company's worksheets, you can simply input the balances from your financial statements into input fields and let the program calculate and prepare cash flow statements using both the indirect and direct methods.

To obtain your Cash Flow Worksheets, visit our internet site.

www.allenandcompanypc.com

Appendix D

Goals Worksheets

You can only realize your dreams after you've defined your goals. Define both financial and non-financial goals. Be specific. Put your goals in writing. Then rank them in order of priority first and then by short-, medium-, or long-term. With Allen & Company's Microsoft Excel Goals Worksheet and Goal Tracking Worksheet, you'll quickly be on your way to defining your goals, prioritizing them, assigning due dates, determining the investment required, and tracking your progress toward accomplishing them.

To obtain your Goals Worksheet and Goal Tracking Worksheet, visit our internet site.

www.allenandcompanypc.com

Appendix E

Industry Review

To compare your company's broad category of expenses to the competitors in your industry when developing your budget or business plan, let Allen & Company provide an Industry Review report. This report also includes various industry financial ratios, growth metrics, and balance sheet ratios. But wait! That's not all! If you order right now, you'll also receive recommendations to improve your company's liquidity, profits, profit margin, and sales!

To obtain your Industry Review, visit our internet site.

www.allenandcompanypc.com

Appendix F

About the Author

Michael R. Allen, CPA

Michael Allen is a certified public accountant (CPA) and founded Allen & Company, PC in November 2006 after recognizing the tremendous opportunity to help individuals and businesses improve their net worth and to achieve their goals. Allen & Company helps hundreds of businesses each year with their accounting and financial statement services. Monthly and quarterly accounting clients receive a complimentary Financial Performance Review at least annually to help them assess the financial health of their businesses.

Additionally, the firm provides business advisory, controller assistance, financial statement audit and review services, and various tax return preparation and planning services.

Prior to starting his firm, Michael worked with international and local CPA firms providing financial statement accounting and assurance, income tax return preparation, and income tax planning services. He also served as a controller in a company that owned and operated quick-service restaurants in Georgia and Alabama.

Michael graduated from the University of Georgia where he earned a bachelor's degree in accounting and a masters degree in accounting systems. Before graduating from graduate school at the University of Georgia, Michael passed the CPA examination on his first attempt. He is also an alumnus of Georgia State University where he earned a masters degree in taxation and where he received the PriceWaterhouseCoopers Tax Research award.

Michael's first job in college was washing dishes, which ended abruptly after two weeks so that he could focus on school and play tennis in the afternoons. Michael's favorite food is Tex Mex and, if he had a second career, it would most likely be as a food and travel critic.

Michael lives in Kennesaw, Georgia with his wife Kristin with their two daughters, Eden and Elise nearby. Over the years, he has enjoyed playing tennis, snow skiing, weight-lifting, reading presidential biographies, and playing piano. Michael, a former Atlanta Falcons season ticket holder, has also been involved in The Georgian Club and drawing and painting classes.

Michael Allen

Appendix G

Contact Us

Allen & Company, PC
1350 Wooten Lake Road, NW
Suite 206
Kennesaw, Georgia 30144

(770) 428-6229 (T)
(770) 425-5481 (F)
mallen@allenandcompanypc.com
www.allenandcompanypc.com

Endnotes

Introduction

[1] Bradley J. Sugars, *Instant Cashflow* (New York: McGraw-Hill Professional, 2006), 8.
[2] Bradley J. Sugars, *Instant Cashflow* (New York: McGraw-Hill Professional, 2006), 7.
[3] Frances McGuckin, *Taking Your Business to the Next Level* (Naperville: Sourcebooks, Inc., 2005), 60.
[4] Jack E. Kinger, Stephen E. Loeb, and Gordon S. May, *Accounting Principles* (New York: Random House, Inc., 1987), 5.

Overview

[1] Committee on Terminology, *Accounting Terminology Bulletins, No. 1 – Review and Resume* (New York: American Institute of Certified Public Accountants, 1961), 9.
[2] Jack E. Kinger, Stephen E. Loeb, and Gordon S. May, *Accounting Principles* (New York: Random House, Inc., 1987), 10-11.

Understanding Balance Sheet Accounts

[1] Committee on Terminology, *Accounting Terminology Bulletins, No. 1 – Review and Resume* (New York: American Institute of Certified Public Accountants, 1961), 12.
[2] Jack E. Kinger, Stephen E. Loeb, and Gordon S. May, *Accounting Principles* (New York: Random House, Inc., 1987), 93.
[3] Jack E. Kinger, Stephen E. Loeb, and Gordon S. May, *Accounting Principles* (New York: Random House, Inc., 1987), 95.
[4] Jack E. Kinger, Stephen E. Loeb, and Gordon S. May, *Accounting Principles* (New York: Random House, Inc., 1987), 14.
[5] Jordan e. Goodman, *Everyone's Money Book* (Chicago: Dearborn Financial Publishing, Inc., 1998), 68.
[6] Jack E. Kinger, Stephen E. Loeb, and Gordon S. May, *Accounting Principles* (New York: Random House, Inc., 1987), 290.
[7] Jack E. Kinger, Stephen E. Loeb, and Gordon S. May, *Accounting Principles* (New York: Random House, Inc., 1987), 300.
[8] Jack E. Kinger, Stephen E. Loeb, and Gordon S. May, *Accounting Principles* (New York: Random House, Inc., 1987), 382.
[9] Jack E. Kinger, Stephen E. Loeb, and Gordon S. May, *Accounting Principles* (New York: Random House, Inc., 1987), 33.
[10] Jack E. Kinger, Stephen E. Loeb, and Gordon S. May, *Accounting Principles* (New York: Random House, Inc., 1987), 267.
[11] Jack E. Kinger, Stephen E. Loeb, and Gordon S. May, *Accounting Principles* (New York: Random House, Inc., 1987), 94.
[12] Jack E. Kinger, Stephen E. Loeb, and Gordon S. May, *Accounting Principles* (New York: Random House, Inc., 1987), 417.
[13] Jack E. Kinger, Stephen E. Loeb, and Gordon S. May, *Accounting Principles* (New York: Random House, Inc., 1987), 419.
[14] Jack E. Kinger, Stephen E. Loeb, and Gordon S. May, *Accounting Principles* (New York: Random House, Inc., 1987), 452.
[15] Jack E. Kinger, Stephen E. Loeb, and Gordon S. May, *Accounting Principles* (New York: Random House, Inc., 1987), 453.
[16] Jack E. Kinger, Stephen E. Loeb, and Gordon S. May, *Accounting Principles* (New York: Random House, Inc., 1987), 94.
[17] Jack E. Kinger, Stephen E. Loeb, and Gordon S. May, *Accounting Principles* (New York: Random House, Inc., 1987), 299.
[18] Jack E. Kinger, Stephen E. Loeb, and Gordon S. May, *Accounting Principles* (New York: Random House, Inc., 1987), 475.
[19] Jack E. Kinger, Stephen E. Loeb, and Gordon S. May, *Accounting Principles* (New York: Random House, Inc., 1987), 474.
[20] Jack E. Kinger, Stephen E. Loeb, and Gordon S. May, *Accounting Principles* (New York: Random House, Inc., 1987), 300.
[21] Jack E. Kinger, Stephen E. Loeb, and Gordon S. May, *Accounting Principles* (New York: Random House, Inc., 1987), 581.
[22] Jack E. Kinger, Stephen E. Loeb, and Gordon S. May, *Accounting Principles* (New York: Random House, Inc., 1987), 582.
[23] Jack E. Kinger, Stephen E. Loeb, and Gordon S. May, *Accounting Principles* (New York: Random House, Inc., 1987), 540-541.
[24] Jack E. Kinger, Stephen E. Loeb, and Gordon S. May, *Accounting Principles* (New York: Random House, Inc., 1987), 612.
[25] Jack E. Kinger, Stephen E. Loeb, and Gordon S. May, *Accounting Principles* (New York: Random House, Inc., 1987), 541.
[26] Jack E. Kinger, Stephen E. Loeb, and Gordon S. May, *Accounting Principles* (New York: Random House, Inc., 1987), 582.

Understanding Income Statement Accounts

Michael Allen

---

[1] Jack E. Kinger, Stephen E. Loeb, and Gordon S. May, *Accounting Principles* (New York: Random House, Inc., 1987), 329.
[2] Jack E. Kinger, Stephen E. Loeb, and Gordon S. May, *Accounting Principles* (New York: Random House, Inc., 1987), 167.

The Recording Process

[1] Frances McGuckin, *Taking Your Business to the Next Level* (Naperville: Sourcebooks, Inc., 2005), 62.
[2] Frances McGuckin, *Taking Your Business to the Next Level* (Naperville: Sourcebooks, Inc., 2005), 63.
[3] G. Thomas Friedlob and Franklin James Plewa, *Understanding Balance Sheets* (New York: New York State Society of CPAs, 1996).
[4] Edrian Henio, *Accounting Numbers as 'Inscription': Action at a Distance and the Development of Accounting* (Cambridge: Accounting, Organizations and Society, 1992), 685-708.
[5] David Oldroyd and Alisdair Dobie, *Themes in the History of Bookkeeping* (London: 2008), 96.
[6] New York Society of CPAs, *A History of Accountancy* (New York: New York State Society of CPAs, 2003).
[7] Michel Thiery, *Did You Say Debit?* (Thailand: Assumption University, 2009), 35.
[8] Albrecht Heefer, *On the Curious Historical Coincidence of Algebra and Double-Entry Bookkeeping* (Ghent: Ghent University, 2009).
[9] Geoffrey A. Lee, *The Coming of Age of Double Entry: The Giovanni Farlfi Ledger* (Oxford: University of Mississippi, 1977), 80.
[10] Alan Sangster, Gret Stoner & Patricia McCarthy, *The Market for Luca Pacioli's Summa Arithmetica* (Cardiff: 2007), 1-2.
[11] Jack E. Kinger, Stephen E. Loeb, and Gordon S. May, *Accounting Principles* (New York: Random House, Inc., 1987), 81.
[12] Jack E. Kinger, Stephen E. Loeb, and Gordon S. May, *Accounting Principles* (New York: Random House, Inc., 1987), 82.
[13] Michael I. Bernstein, Joan W. Grey, and G. Douglas Puckett, *PPC's 1120 Deskbook* (Fort Worth: Thomson Tax & Accounting, 2007), 3-2 – 3-4.

The Closing Process

[1] Jack E. Kinger, Stephen E. Loeb, and Gordon S. May, *Accounting Principles* (New York: Random House, Inc., 1987), 36.
[2] Jack E. Kinger, Stephen E. Loeb, and Gordon S. May, *Accounting Principles* (New York: Random House, Inc., 1987), 120.
[3] Jack E. Kinger, Stephen E. Loeb, and Gordon S. May, *Accounting Principles* (New York: Random House, Inc., 1987), 53.
[4] Jack E. Kinger, Stephen E. Loeb, and Gordon S. May, *Accounting Principles* (New York: Random House, Inc., 1987), 48.

Understanding Financial Statements

[1] Jack E. Kinger, Stephen E. Loeb, and Gordon S. May, *Accounting Principles* (New York: Random House, Inc., 1987), 92.
[2] Aric Jenkins, *Warren Buffett's Net Worth Has Reached a Staggering New High* (New York: Time, Inc., 2017).
[3] Jack E. Kinger, Stephen E. Loeb, and Gordon S. May, *Accounting Principles* (New York: Random House, Inc., 1987), 772.
[4] Jack E. Kinger, Stephen E. Loeb, and Gordon S. May, *Accounting Principles* (New York: Random House, Inc., 1987), 756.
[5] Jack E. Kinger, Stephen E. Loeb, and Gordon S. May, *Accounting Principles* (New York: Random House, Inc., 1987), 760.
[6] Edward M. Hynes & Walt K. Matysik, *PPC's Guide to Restaurants and Bars* (Fort Worth: Thomson Tax & Accounting, 2013), 3-14.
[7] Jack E. Kinger, Stephen E. Loeb, and Gordon S. May, *Accounting Principles* (New York: Random House, Inc., 1987), 900-901.
[8] Paul Dunn and Ron Baker, *The Firm of the Future* (Hoboken: John Wiley & Sons, Inc., 2003), 229.
[9] Paul Dunn and Ron Baker, *The Firm of the Future* (Hoboken: John Wiley & Sons, Inc., 2003), 232.
[10] Paul Dunn and Ron Baker, *The Firm of the Future* (Hoboken: John Wiley & Sons, Inc., 2003), 241-242.
[11] Paul Dunn and Ron Baker, *The Firm of the Future* (Hoboken: John Wiley & Sons, Inc., 2003), 242-243.
[12] Paul Dunn and Ron Baker, *The Firm of the Future* (Hoboken: John Wiley & Sons, Inc., 2003), 243-244.
[13] Paul Dunn and Ron Baker, *The Firm of the Future* (Hoboken: John Wiley & Sons, Inc., 2003), 244-245.
[14] Paul Dunn and Ron Baker, *The Firm of the Future* (Hoboken: John Wiley & Sons, Inc., 2003), 245-249.
[15] Jack E. Kinger, Stephen E. Loeb, and Gordon S. May, *Accounting Principles* (New York: Random House, Inc., 1987), 750.
[16] Jack E. Kinger, Stephen E. Loeb, and Gordon S. May, *Accounting Principles* (New York: Random House, Inc., 1987), 751.
[17] Jack E. Kinger, Stephen E. Loeb, and Gordon S. May, *Accounting Principles* (New York: Random House, Inc., 1987), 752-753.

[18] Jack E. Kinger, Stephen E. Loeb, and Gordon S. May, *Accounting Principles* (New York: Random House, Inc., 1987), 1062-1068.
[19] Jack E. Kinger, Stephen E. Loeb, and Gordon S. May, *Accounting Principles* (New York: Random House, Inc., 1987), 1069.
[20] Jack E. Kinger, Stephen E. Loeb, and Gordon S. May, *Accounting Principles* (New York: Random House, Inc., 1987), 1069.

Preparing Budgets and Forecasts

[1] Jack E. Kinger, Stephen E. Loeb, and Gordon S. May, *Accounting Principles* (New York: Random House, Inc., 1987), 916.
[2] Dave Ramsey, *The Total Money Makeover* (Nashville: Thomas Nelson, Inc., 2007), 97.
[3] Jack E. Kinger, Stephen E. Loeb, and Gordon S. May, *Accounting Principles* (New York: Random House, Inc., 1987), 916.
[4] Jack E. Kinger, Stephen E. Loeb, and Gordon S. May, *Accounting Principles* (New York: Random House, Inc., 1987), 919.
[5] Jack E. Kinger, Stephen E. Loeb, and Gordon S. May, *Accounting Principles* (New York: Random House, Inc., 1987), 920-921.
[6] Jack E. Kinger, Stephen E. Loeb, and Gordon S. May, *Accounting Principles* (New York: Random House, Inc., 1987), 921.

9 7 9 8 9 9 9 1 6 0 4 0 9